HIP
HOTELS

SKI

HERBERT YPMA

HIP
HOTELS

SKI

with 511 illustrations, 379 in color

Thames & Hudson

introduction

The first time my grandfather took my grandmother skiing, she hated it. They went to Schruns in Austria, in those days a favourite of Hemingway. The journey was long and slow, but this was the part of the vacation that my grandmother enjoyed. Once in the mountains, it was a different story. Their suitcases were thrown unceremoniously onto a mule-drawn hay cart, and when their horse-drawn sleigh arrived at the bottom of a steep mountain-face, guests were instructed to strap skins on their skis and 'skin' their way up to the hotel. My grandma wasn't having any of it – frozen, tired and as stubborn as the mules that were pulling her luggage, she wouldn't move another inch. But the track was too steep for the horses, and another solution had to be found. The hotel did have a crude cable-lift of sorts – a wooden box, to be exact, used to haul up supplies. So my grandmother, together with luggage and groceries, was put in it and winched to the hotel kitchen. It was her first and last ski vacation.

How skiing has changed. It used to be all exertion and intrepid adventure – now it's strictly all fun. High-speed lifts whisk skiers to altitudes previously reserved for serious alpinists, and linked ski areas make it possible not just to ski to another village but, in certain parts of the Alps, to other countries and back again. Fresh snow is produced artificially during the night, and slopes are groomed like best bowling lawns. Even the most basic hotels offer all the comforts of home and more.

But somehow, I can't help feeling a sense of loss: the loss of adventure, of discovery and of the thrill of escape to different cultures. At one time, the Austrians with their *Lederhosen* and *Dirndl*, their felt shoes and huge horns, would have seemed as exotic as the Balinese. Now, many of those traditions have become tourist window dressing for the package-holiday crowd. As a keen skier, I understand there is a price to pay for today's technical marvels; but I'm also an idealist and I refuse to accept that all the more rewarding aspects of travel have to be sacrificed in the name of a good day's skiing.

The truth is, they don't. This book features ski hotels in Europe and North America where the experience goes beyond a day's vertical. And there are more than you might imagine. They range from a centuries-old farmhouse in a forgotten Austrian valley to Robert Redford's ski ranch in Utah; organic sixties architecture to a collection of wilderness lakeside log cabins. Romantics and idealists take heart: skiing *can* still offer adventure as well as sport.

hotel eden

Not only was it snowing heavily when I arrived, but everything was shrouded in a thick white mist – a case of blanc on blanc. The first thing my eyes picked out was an old refrigerator on a pedestal with the name 'Kitchen Club' handpainted on the door. As I was to discover, that old fridge was a fair emblem for the hotel.

The Kitchen Club is Hotel Eden's nightclub, and the basement where it is located was the original kitchen of this Swiss former sanatorium. But when they say at the Eden that the disco is in the kitchen, they really mean in the kitchen. People dance on stoves, the stainless steel sinks are used for serving drinks, and whatever old kitchen appliance is not used as a table serves as impromptu sculpture.

Next door in the basement is Jungle Jim, a comprehensive sauna, aerobics room, massage centre and weights gym. With a silver-panelled ceiling, a wild collection of palms and tropical plants, bamboo furniture and a leopardskin tablecloth, it's all a bit kitsch. But it's meant to be. The Eden's only convention is the unconventional way it presents itself. Take the breakfast room, a grand affair with panoramic windows overlooking Arosa's mountains. Its exposed concrete grid ceiling is painted Yves Klein blue, chairs are imitation Louis IV

upholstered in bright red, blue, yellow and green, and they sit under a huge, crudely made chandelier that can only be described as 'backyard baroque'. Even the paper napkins and the breakfast bowls are in a rainbow range of bold colours.

The Eden is like the product of an ideas brainstorming session gone haywire. There are electric street surfers in the lobby for guests to zip around town and an in-house Italian restaurant that mimics the corny grotto style so favoured by Italian emigrants. Yet another dining room takes the blue-and-white gingham of traditional mountain resorts and throws it around as if it had been tied to a mountain goat let loose in the room. But where the Eden has really chucked out the baby with the bathwater is in the hotel services guide. I didn't even know for sure if it *was* the services guide – it's colourful and textural enough to entertain a baby for hours. It includes a piece of carpet whose tartan plaid matches that on the floor of the bar. There's a plastic page half-filled with water (the pool) and white powder (the skiing piste), a black and white plastified photo of a naked butt (the gym), and a piece of blue bubble-wrap whose meaning I still haven't worked out.

Nowhere is the Eden's three-dimensional expression session more uninhibited than on the fourth floor. These aren't rooms but zones where ideas were allowed to germinate like mushrooms. When you talk to proprietor Hitsch Leu about the Tiger Lily room, he smiles politely as if putting a bed in a cage, decorating the walls with circus posters and covering furniture with *faux* leopardskin were perfectly commonplace. Still, compared with room 408, it's tame (no pun intended). A bronze tree growing out of the corner of the room – OK. A jacuzzi set in a raised *faux* grotto decorated with broken tiles à la Gaudi – fine. A stereo system in a stack of Fred Flintstone boulders – sure. But bedquilts cut and shaped and stitched to resemble two giant leaves – now we're talking strange. The idea of these rooms was to provide something for everyone, and come to think of it, that's pretty much the theme for the entire hotel. In German, they call it a hotel for the *Leute von Heute* (loyta fon hoyta) – the people of today.

As with most successful creativity, however, behind the scenes there is a great deal of care and discipline. The alien-like candlesticks in the gingham-gone-berserk restaurant were designed to hold a candle and a green apple. There were no green apples the day I was photographing, but the restaurant manager almost had a fit when I suggested lemons instead. 'No no no,' he said, 'that's all wrong. It's supposed to be a green apple – that's how it was designed. I cannot let you photograph it with lemons.' Only after much negotiation did we settle on green capsicums instead.

Like the Eden, Arosa is a bit of a surprise too. I had no idea the village is so high – 1,800 metres (5,900 feet). In the middle of April it was still snowing. It's a snow-safe resort, but it's not without its trials to get there. When you see the sign in Chur, 30-odd kilometres seems like nothing – until you start to negotiate the 1,583 turns along the way. The last sign says 'six more curves until Arosa' – as if they guessed you were on the point of giving up hope.

---

address   Hotel Eden, 7050 Arosa, Switzerland

t +41 (81) 378 7100   **f** +41 (81) 378 7101   **e** info@edenarosa.ch

room rates from SFr 140

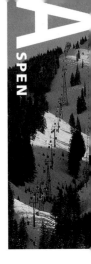
aspen meadows

Bauhaus in the snow: simple streamlined architecture, big wide spaces unencumbered by superfluous decoration, floor to ceiling windows that frame idyllic mountain views, every design detail conceived as a partner of function… usually the tenets of Bauhaus teaching are a utopian ideal, but at Aspen Meadows the Bauhaus model comes closer to being realized without compromise than anywhere else on this planet where there is snow.

The Bauhaus school in Weimar Germany was the powerhouse of modernism. Breuer, Gropius, Mies van der Rohe and their peers spearheaded a movement founded on the conviction that architecture and design could help create a better life. The Bauhaus approach to town planning was to group buildings together in dense configuration, so that the surrounding space could be devoted to parks, trees and recreational facilities. Bauhaus professors, however, generally failed to anticipate the mindset of all the property developers who have subsequently used that leftover space to put up more buildings. At Aspen Meadows, this was not the case. Its hundred-odd rooms are set in a forty-acre park of meandering streams, footpaths, wooden bridges and ponds, and all in a location that

commands an impressive view of Aspen's ski mountains. Throughout the complex, inside and out, the emphasis is on space. The rooms, by ordinary hotel standards, are huge. In fact they are apartments, each and every one of them, with a separate bedroom, bathroom, kitchen, living room and study area. Entire walls of glass bring the mountains into your room and even in the darkest winter months an impressive amount of daylight is reflected off the snow into the sand-and-white interior.

The predominant architectural heritage of Aspen expresses its origins as a mining settlement, and most of the more elaborate accommodation in town offers rather dark and plush Victorian interiors. This may be historically sympathetic, but frankly I think the natural beauty of the area should take priority. In the architecture of Aspen Meadows, it does. In any case, in a resort filled with Prada, Gucci, Chanel and Christian Dior boutiques, not to mention an airport stacked with gleaming private jets, pursuing a Victorian mining town aesthetic seems incongruous if not bizarre.

It's no surprise to discover that the founder of Aspen Meadows was more concerned with inventing a dynamic and forward-looking cultural centre than preserving a historic town.

15

Floor-to-ceiling glass walls bring in plenty of daylight to accent the restrained beige and white colour scheme

White birch trees and panels of red and yellow create a powerful modernist statement in the snow

Each guest suite has a kitchen and a separate living area – more like an apartment than a hotel room

The view from Aspen Meadows takes in three peaks of Aspen: Ajax, Buttermilk and Aspen Highlands

The dining room is a big, bright, minimal glass box furnished with 'Hoop' chairs designed by Frank Gehry

Aspen Meadow's unapologetically modern architecture sits comfortably in its pristine white winter environment

aspen meadows

The vision Chicago industrialist Walter Paepcke had for Aspen was of a place where the world's greatest thinkers, artists and leaders would gather and be inspired by the magnificent nature surrounding them. He hired Bauhaus-trained Austrian architect Herbert Bayer to make his dream a three-dimensional reality. In the end, Bayer didn't have as much of an influence on the town as his patron would have liked, but at Aspen Meadows he certainly achieved most of the loftiest of Bauhaus ideals.

Situated on the outskirts of town, Aspen Meadows is close enough to nip in for dinner or shopping, but far away enough for you to be conscious always of why Aspen is such a magnet – namely the beauty of the mountains and the superb quality of the skiing. Staying here is an experience completely unlike that of any ski hotel I have been to. On the one hand the layout is campus-like: pathways link one pavilion to the next, meandering past works of contemporary art. But there is also a futuristic, surreal quality to the place. Perhaps

it is the softly spoken staff, the lack of noise, the pristine cleanliness, or the electric cars that give Meadows a *Man From U.N.C.L.E.* quality. This rarefied 'I Spy' atmosphere is due to the fact that Aspen Meadows is part of the Aspen Institute – the broad-based think-tank founded by Paepcke that counts some of the world's most influential people on its board. At different times of the year you may find George Bush Sr. or Bill Koch, statesmen or captains of industry staying in rooms otherwise occupied by powder hounds. For despite Aspen's ritzy reputation, this is also America's premier ski resort. And that's not because there is an impressive new Prada shop on Galena Street, but because Aspen Mountain, Aspen Highlands, Buttermilk, and Snowmass offer a choice and a lack of crowds that cannot easily be matched elsewhere. Forget the private jets, the big-city real estate prices, the *chichi* restaurants – what really counts is that, bar Whistler, Snowmass has more vertical than any other ski resort in North America.

address Aspen Meadows, 845 Meadows Road, Aspen, Colorado 81611, USA

t +1 (970) 925 4240 **f** +1 (970) 925 7790 **e** keith.sexton@aspenmeadows.com

room rates from US $89

the brand

Aspen started life as a silver-mining town in the late 1870s in Colorado's Roaring Fork Valley. For years it was nothing more than a camp, a collection of rickety timber shacks that offered little protection from either the vicious weather or the marauding bands of local Ute Indians. The pioneering prospectors persevered nonetheless and by the late 1880s Aspen had a population of twelve thousand. The town could boast two railways, no fewer than six newspapers, three schools, ten churches, and an impressively large red light district. Then the silver market collapsed and so did the town.

The second coming of Aspen has been well documented, perhaps too well. Celebrity-obsessed magazines have even scrutinized the parking pecking order of the gleaming private jets lined up in Aspen's jet park. If you don't have the latest G5 you can forget having your plane out front. The same pecking-order access applies in bars with VIP rooms (in a ski resort, for goodness sake) and in restaurants that automatically reserve the best tables for any A-list celebrity who happens to be in town. Then there's the shopping. Aspen has over two hundred boutiques that proudly claim to have the merchandise to push almost any platinum card over its limit.

No wonder Aspen is often dismissed as too glitzy, too expensive and too jet-set. Despite the gloss, however, many serious skiers still count Aspen as their favourite American resort. That's because it offers extraordinary potential for all levels of skiers, on a par with major resorts such as Whistler in Canada or Les Trois Vallées in France. The area comprises four separate mountains. Aspen Mountain or Ajax, as it is known, in the centre of town is an advanced mountain whose runs are all black or double-black diamond. Buttermilk, on the other hand, is perfect for beginners and intermediates, and all its runs are wide, perfectly groomed cruising pistes. Aspen Highlands is a mountain for skiers who prefer their pleasure off-piste, and Snowmass is a combination of all three, with the added distinction of having the longest continuous vertical in the US. Most surprising of all is the lack of crowds. In Europe's equivalent jet-set destinations, lift queues are simply part of the local scene. But Aspen is too remote to be accessible to day-skiers from Denver (who flock instead to Copper Mountain, Breckenridge, and Vail), and its terrain is so large and so well serviced by a network of lifts that it can absorb a considerable number of skiers before becoming congested.

So the message is: avoid the shopping and enjoy Aspen for its beauty and its immaculate slopes. Yet ironically it was the shopping that led me to the tiny but luxuriously different hotel called the Brand. Ask most Aspen regulars to to name a hotel and they will inevitably mention The Nell or Hotel Jerome. One is a quasi-contemporary, outrageously expensive celebrity cauldron on the base of Mount Ajax; the other is a dark old Victorian hotel decorated in a robber baron version of Liberty floral overkill. Mention the Brand and you will most likely get a blank stare.

It's not surprising no one has heard of it – it doesn't even have a sign outside. The entrance is a discreet glass door in the middle of a row of very upmarket shops – right between Gucci and Dior, to be exact. Up a carpeted flight of stairs there's no obvious reception desk, no bar, no public space to speak of. Not many hotels try this hard to disguise themselves. But the Brand is for the Aspen skier who prefers discretion to extravagance,

low-key sophistication to high-profile excess. The Brand's luxury is in the individuality and scale of the accommodation it offers. Its six apartments are decorated according to different themes, all dreamed up by Harley Baldwin, an Aspen resident who started out selling crêpes in the 1960s and ended up as the town's premier landlord. Gucci, Dior and Fendi are just some of his tenants in this darkly imposing Victorian box of a building. It was his success as a landlord that allowed Harley to indulge in the decorative fantasy upstairs. Together with designer Peter Hans Kunz, he travelled to antique markets, fairs, and auctions all over the world to collect the hoard with which they have furnished the Brand: Oriental rugs, Art Deco armchairs, Scandinavian pine furniture, Native American blankets, primitive pots, drums, terracotta lamps and modern art. The result is a delightfully rampant eclecticism that seems not at all out of place when you discover that these spaces once housed the studios of Lichtenstein, Warhol and Christo.

address The Brand Building, 205 S. Galena Street, Aspen, Colorado 81611, USA

t +1 (970) 920 1800 **f** +1 (970) 920 3602 **e** bilstolz@rof.net

room rates from US $365

le mas de la coutettaz

Even in the best-preserved villages of the Haute Savoie, it's not so easy to come across a completely untouched farmhouse. Truth is when I first saw Le Mas de la Coutettaz I had no idea it was a hotel. I was on a real-estate expedition, and was briefly convinced this was one of those properties you read about in a Peter Mayle book – the perfect, slightly dilapidated farmhouse, full of potential, which everyone seems to have overlooked. I was all prepared to knock on the door and enquire whether this gem was for sale, but first I was going to have a good look around outside. To the people inside it must have appeared peculiar – a stranger nosing around like a council worker looking for an electricity meter. So they did what obviously came naturally to them: they put their heads outside and asked if I would like a brochure.

Damn! Someone had beaten me to it, and by such a margin that they had already converted to a hotel. I almost found myself hoping it would be terrible – that the house would punish the wrong owner for failing to convert sensitively. No such luck. The new proprietor had the good taste to change as little as possible, and thus to retain the rare charm of such an authentic Haute Savoie farmhouse.

Dorrien Ricardo knows Morzine very well. For many years he was the local director of a British tour company. He saw in the town the qualities of a genuine community with roots that go back long before the ski boom hit the mountains, and in the ski area he saw a potential that is consistently overlooked and underrated by conventional guidebooks. Morzine, they will tell you, is a charming town set in wooded mountains with a river running through it, but for skiing it's too low, with unreliable snow and potentially patchy cover. Not true! The close proximity of Mont Blanc and its neighbouring sky-high peaks creates a microclimate of sorts. There's always more snow here than in other parts of the French Alps at the same altitude, and since the valleys are also narrow and dark and not south-facing, it hangs around a lot longer.

Morzine is usually lumped into the giant Portes du Soleil ski area, an enormous linked terrain that includes Châtel, Chavanette, Champéry, Champoussin, Les Lindarets and Morgins, and darts up and down and in and out of nearby Switzerland. And while it's true that it's relatively straightforward to take the gondola in town to the high-altitude resort of Avoriaz and from there access the variety and

magnitude of the Portes du Soleil, there's also an almost overlooked series of mountains on Morzine's doorstep that provide a peaceful and crowd-free alternative. During the week you practically have these mountains to yourself, which as any regular Alpine skier knows, is a rare treat, particularly in France. Even on weekends you're unlikely to encounter a queue because the weekend crowd from Geneva prefer to go to Avoriaz. And for the skier who likes the idea of skiing *to* somewhere – of making a journey with a proper destination – there aren't many places better suited. On a typical day, you might start at 2,020-metre (6,600 foot) Pointe de Nyon, and proceed in a counter-clockwise direction down to Le Grand Pré, up again to Chamossière, over to Le Ranfolly, down to Les Chavannes, then down to the village of Les Gets, up to the peak of Mont Chéry and then via the lifts at Le Pléney back down to Morzine.

With its profitable slate quarries, Morzine was one of few Alpine villages not solely dependent on farming in the days before skiing. As the traditional roofing material of the Alps, slate was good business, and it was slate money that built Le Mas de la Coutettaz. Situated in one of the best spots in town, just above the church and the river that runs alongside it, the property was originally built for a gentleman farmer who had made his fortune from slate. The ground floor is still lined with enormous, well-oiled, gleaming black slabs of it, a legacy to his success and to the town's pre-skiing economy.

Not only has the age-old Savoyard character and ambience of the house been preserved, but it is complemented by the cheerful informality of staying here. Dinner as well as breakfast is included in the room rate, and food is served at a single giant candlelit table in the former stables.

Alas, it's true, the old farmhouse makes a splendid hotel – authentic and full of charm. But, selfishly, it would have made me an even more amazing house. Maybe next time.

address Le Mas de la Coutettaz, Chemin de la Coutettaz, 74110 Morzine, France

t +33 (4) 5079 0826 **f** +33 (4) 5079 1853 **e** info@thefarmhouse.co.uk

room rates from €190

les dromonts

Perched on top of a sheer cliff that plunges more than a thousand feet into a narrow valley below, the ski town of Avoriaz is like nothing else in France or, for that matter, the world. Avoriaz is like a modernist Californian version of *The Eagle has Landed*. Take away the Schloss and Clint Eastwood and Richard Burton in white uniforms, keep the eagle's eyrie position, and you have some idea of the spectacle of this setting.

Forty years ago the town of Avoriaz didn't exist. This was high summer pasture for the farmers from nearby Morzine, and Avoriaz was still just an idea in the mind of a Paris-based property developer. His dream was to build the equivalent of St Tropez in the snow – young, sexy and ultra-hip. And like Port Grimaud around the corner from St Trop, it was to be architecturally consistent. The town was envisaged with no traffic, just horsedrawn sleighs; no roads, just snow-covered tracks; and lots and lots of timber. It's not often that one architect gets to design a whole town, and even less often at an altitude of 1,800 metres (6,000 feet) in the French Alps. And what a town it turned out to be. The form of the buildings echoes the sheer faces of brown slate that they sit on, and from a distance the staggered

heights of the multi-storey structures blend perfectly into the extraordinary dynamism of the area's topography. Architect Jacques Labro's very first building in what became the distinct Avoriaz style was Les Dromonts. Three and half decades ago, this hotel set the architectural pace for the design of the entire resort. It was totally new and totally innovative. The resort of Avoriaz soon became the hottest snow destination in flower-power France. Rock stars bought apartments, media personalities wanted to be seen here, and the money men were smacking their lips.

But eventually the fickle finger of fashion started to point back towards tradition, and Avoriaz lost its edge. The town did not suffer too much, however: the numerous apartment buildings stayed full, and the surrounding ski slopes were developed into one of Europe's largest and most extensive linked areas, the Portes du Soleil. Skiers no longer came because it was a 'scene' but because they could ski to Châtel, to Champéry in Switzerland, and back again. The entire town, still car-free, is ski in, ski out. 'Wake up in the morning, step into your skis and go' remains its mantra. No traffic means it is perfect for children and the altitude makes it reliably snow-safe.

The unique and completely consistent aesthetic of Avoriaz reflects the fact that it was all designed by one architect

Perched on the edge of a spectacular cliff, Avoriaz has one of the most breathtaking locations in the world

Guestrooms avoid the 'boring box' configuration by the interaction of unexpected angles and unusual space

From the hotel's signature porthole windows the view takes in the Alpine setting of the Portes du Soleil ski area

The hotel's architecture is funky sixties at its best: organic, free-flowing, and full of intersecting planes and curves

Chef Christophe Leroy opened two hotel restaurants – the casual à la carte (above) and the gourmand (below)

Ironically the only building that did suffer in Avoriaz's metamorphosis from hip town to ski town was the Hôtel des Dromonts. Once upon a time it had been the architectural trailblazer. The terrace construction, the timber cladding, the porthole windows, and the distinctive granite-peak shape were invented for Les Dromonts and then reinterpreted for all the other multi-storey buildings of Avoriaz. But as this became a town of apartment dwellers, so the hotel slid into irrelevance and disrepair. A lot of the locals who had stayed on from the early days were frustrated by its decline; their own guests no longer had anywhere decent to stay. It seemed a sad and hopeless story until a successful hotelier from St Tropez stepped in to save the day. Christophe Leroy has a bit of an eye for what people want and a feel for where taste is heading. He recognized in Les Dromonts something that others had failed to see – not just inspiring and highly original organic sixties architecture, but a buzz just waiting to be revived.

After an eighteen-month renovation Les Dromonts was ready to reopen. Leroy is responsible for a lot of what the hotel now has to offer – the food, for instance, is of a standard more often found in sophisticated French cities. But just as importantly he did very little to the existing architecture. The asymmetrical organic curves, the circular windows, and the riot of intersecting walls at peculiar angles are still as they were in the sixties. Guestrooms all have new bathrooms, but the rooms themselves retain the asymmetry and unlikely angles that distinguish the lobby and other public spaces. And the buzz is back. Locals often drop in for a drink, and the hotel's two restaurants are continually booked.

Les Dromonts is an architectural experience like no other in the snow. While Californians are busy rediscovering the modernist architecture of Neutra and Schindler, the French are finally rekindling their love affair with the bold and adventurous architectural spirit of the 1960s.

address Les Dromonts, Quartier des Dromonts, 74110 Avoriaz, France
t +33 (4) 5074 0811   **f** +33 (4) 5074 0279   **e** leroych83@aol.com
room rates from €276

grüner baum

The history of Grüner Baum (or green tree) starts, appropriately enough, with a green rebel. Archduke Johann, known to historians as the house of Hapsburg's green rebel because of his love of forests, laid the foundations of a hunting lodge in 1831 in the Kötschach Valley, gateway to what is today the Hohe Tauern national park. While society women took the healing waters of nearby Badgastein, their men would go to hunt in the Kötschachtal. Over the next half a dozen decades, the lodge became a favourite retreat among the most prominent of the Bad guests.

European aristocrats and royals have been coming to bathe in the hot springs of Badgastein for almost five centuries, and the town today has the same sort of grand turn-of-the-century architecture that graces spas like Baden-Baden and Evian. Grüner Baum, however, despite its grand history, was still a rustic lodge in the Prossau Alps at the beginning of the twentieth century. Then in 1913 it was acquired by the family of the present proprietors, and slowly, almost organically, the personality of Grüner Baum as a hotel started to take shape.

Despite many setbacks, including a major fire that destroyed everything in 1923, Grüner Baum had one magical ingredient that could never be taken away – its extraordinary location. Judging from historic photographs, the Kötschachtal has changed not one bit. Grüner Baum's modern conveniences are more elaborate, to be sure, but both the architecture and the surrounding nature are untouched. Situated at the entrance to the Hohe Tauern national park, the Kötschachtal is protected from developers not by the authorities but by the fact that the entire valley is owned by one family. All that you see in this idyllic *Sound of Music* setting belongs to the Blumschein family. Monica Blumschein grew up in the Kötschach valley and not only does she love it, she talks about it with such animated conviction that you would think she had only just arrived. But then its beauty is spellbinding. This is the kind of perfect Alpine spot that can't fail to conjure up wholesome Singing Nun fantasies.

Grüner Baum is not just a hotel but a *Hoteldorf*. The entire village is your host, and every building you see is part of the experience of staying there. Accommodation includes the main house, the Land House, the Jäger House, the Kössler House, and the Lindy House. These five different buildings afford a variety of different ways to stay. The main house is perfect for devotees of traditional Austrian style.

Details like this typically Austrian painted door contribute to Grüner Baum's captivating authenticity

Rustic wooden panelling in the guestrooms reflects the traditional Austrian values of the Blumschein family

Grüner Baum's Alpine surroundings are still as wild as when this was a royal hunting lodge in the 1800s

The original *Stube* survives intact from the early 1900s. This funky Baroque *Kachel* stands in the corner of the room

Horsedrawn sleighs are ideal for making excursions into the picturesque and unspoilt Kötschach Valley

The *Hoteldorf* or village includes a tiny chapel, three guesthouses, an old ski shop, a big barn…and nothing else

The Land House is good for families, Lindy is self-catered apartments, Jäger House contains the standard (less expensive) rooms, and Kössler House is ideal for guests keen to make use of the extensive spa facilities.

The entrance to the national park is right on your doorstep. In winter, when the valley is blanketed in snow, guests can take a horsedrawn sleigh into the Prossau. But aside from the splendid setting, the perfect back-to-nature isolation of the Kötschachtal, and all the 'here I am, spoil me rotten' features – indoor heated pool, two restaurants, numerous private dining rooms, radon baths, massages, Shiseido skin treatment – the most convincing attraction of Grüner Baum remains its unaffected Austrian charm. The staff are never out of their *Loden*, *Lederhosen* or *Dirndl*, the main house still has its original *Stube* complete with the most exotic *Kachel* stove I've seen. And every detail, from the pastries served in the afternoon by the fire to the exterior colour scheme, celebrates the traditions of Austria.

Grüner Baum makes a wonderful retreat at any time of year, but it also happens to be perfect for skiers. Cross-country skiers only have to step outside the front door – exquisitely picturesque trails start just behind the main house and continue into the park. For downhill skiers there's a shuttle to the various slopes of the Badgastein ski area. The only decision you need to make is which Gastein? Badhofgastein, Dorfgastein, Sportgastein (favourite with the Blumschein family), or of course Badgastein, not to mention smaller slopes such as the nearby Graukogel (five minutes by car).

The mountains, the family, the traditions – you just can't stop recalling *The Sound of Music*. Particularly when you discover that Erna Linsinger, who together with Monica's father Erwin Linsinger instigated Grüner Baum's transition from simple inn to sophisticated retreat, started her life with some strict schooling in a convent in Salzburg, where one of her teachers was none other than the future Baroness von Trapp, aka the Singing Nun.

---

address Grüner Baum, Kötschachtal 25, A–5640 Badgastein, Austria

t +43 (643) 425 160 **f** +43 (643) 425 1625 **e** info@grunerbaum.com

room rates from €105

buffalo mountain lodge

In the late 1800s Canada's leaders knew that if the young nation was to maintain its claim to the lands of its wild and unpopulated west, they would have to link them to the more urban and densely populated east. Their solution was one of the most impressive engineering feats of Victorian times, and one of the most expensive. The Canadian Pacific Railway was threatening to bankrupt the nation until William Cornelius Van Horne, its visionary head, decided to cash in on Canada's chief asset. Van Horne was one of the first to recognize that Canada contains some of the world's most impressive wilderness. Build a resort, he reasoned, and people will use the railway to visit it. And they did, in huge numbers. Banff Springs, a spectacularly situated site with natural hot springs, was a popular destination. In time, Banff grew into a beautiful little town in its own right. To protect the country's assets for future generations, the Canadian government established the National Parks Authority, and in 1885 the area of Banff became Canada's first national park.

Calgary-based Pat and Constance O'Connor, proprietors of Rocky Mountain Resorts, know a thing or two about dealing with Canada's National Parks Authority. They purchased their first mountain resort, Emerald Lake Lodge,

more than twenty years ago. Canada Parks had served notice that the lodge would no longer be allowed to operate. The lakeside diesel generators were noisy and leaky, and the lodge itself was, in the words of its new proprietors, 'at the opposite end of functional, let alone luxury'. The O'Connors survived a severe economic downturn, a complete project overhaul and seemingly endless negotiations with Canada Parks before they were able to reopen. A lesser couple would have given up. But not only has their business thrived, with Deer Lodge and Buffalo Mountain Lodge following the success of Emerald Lake Lodge, they have also become staunch supporters of the national parks. They firmly believe that Canada's mountain sanctuaries are without equal, and this conviction is reflected in the great care and empathy they bring to the planning of their hotels. Even the food they serve at Buffalo Mountain Lodge – local game, indigenous berries, wild fruits – is sourced from a ranch they have established outside Calgary to provide authentic ingredients for their mountain restaurants.

Buffalo Mountain Lodge (so named because the mountain it sits on was said by indigenous peoples to resemble a buffalo lying down) is a

timber and fieldstone complex on the slopes of Tunnel Mountain, overlooking the town of Banff and the extraordinarily picturesque Bow Valley. Built in the post and beam style, this mountain retreat is completely in harmony with its surroundings. Rooms achieve a rugged effect without props or paraphernalia, just a large fieldstone fireplace in the corner, two Adirondack chairs, and lots of exposed timber. They are both sober and quite luxurious – in a low-key way. Hiding in a large timber cupboard for instance is a gigantic cable television. Heating is under the floor, and the bathroom is large enough for a clawfoot bath and a separate shower booth. Balance is what the O'Connors are particularly good at.

Banff, however, is not a ski resort, and you must start your skiing day by taking a bus: not ideal, though it does mean you have a choice of skiing destinations. The nearest mountain is a small family resort called Norquay – pretty as a button, it won't win awards for challenging skiing, but it has a charm that has long since disappeared from most ski resorts. Further afield (a twenty-five minute drive) is Sunshine Mountain, famous for having the best snow in Canada. Until recently, Sunshine was an intermediate resort with one major drawback: a very slow gondola that transports skiers to the main village. All that has changed with a new gondola reputed to be the fastest in the northern hemisphere, and the completely new development of Goatshead, an all black and double-black diamond mountain. Also within easy reach of Banff are Lake Louise, Kicking Horse (a brand-new mountain development) and Nakiska, site of the Calgary Olympics.

Like most things in life, staying at Buffalo Mountain Lodge is a trade-off. Commuting to the slopes is an inconvenience – but the food, the ambience and the architecture are all wholly in sympathy with a setting that is among the most picturesque in the world. I don't like getting into a bus first thing in the morning, but if it means Banff will be just as beautiful a hundred years from now then it's worth it.

address Buffalo Mountain Lodge, Tunnel Mountain Road, PO Box 1326, Banff, Alberta, Canada, T1L 1B3

t +1 (403) 609 6150 **f** +1 (403) 609 6158 **e** info@crmr.com

room rates from Cdn $159

the post

It's amazing what you can learn from a bus driver. 'Where are you staying?' he inquired, as we pulled away from Calgary airport, destination Lake Louise. 'The Post,' I replied. His eyes lit up and he launched into an animated account of how I was staying at one of the best hotels in western Canada, with what was in his opinion the best restaurant in all of Canada. During the two and a half hour drive, I got the full rundown on the hotel and its proprietors, including the fact that one of them gets a brand new red Ferrari every two years.

The story of the Post starts with two Swiss ski instructors who came to the Canadian Rockies just to take a look, and never left. For many years André Schwarz ran the ski school at Lake Louise while his brother George retired from teaching and went into the restaurant business in nearby Banff. The two remained closely connected to the Lake Louise community, and when the owner of a small log cabin compound along the river let it be known that he'd be willing to sell, they wasted no time. Sir Norman Watson, a British aircraft manufacturer, was a legendary figure here who loved this part of the Rockies more than anywhere. He was a great ambassador for the Canadian mountains and his primary

consideration in selling his property was that it should not be spoilt by inappropriate development. In André and George Schwarz, he knew he had two purchasers in whom he could have complete confidence. The parcel of land the two brothers took over included not just the group of cabins but also a hotel of a nondescript architecture. For the first seven years, they ran the place without making many changes. They certainly had plans of all kinds for improvements and additions – but first they had to convince the National Parks Authority. The site they had purchased from Sir Norman was the only piece of privately held land in the entire preserved wilderness, and Canada Parks refused to permit any development, certainly not on the scale the Schwarz brothers had in mind. But eventually a solution to the stand-off was found, and it involved some good old-fashioned horsetrading: the ex-ski instructors got their planning permission in return for giving back all rights to the land. Canada Parks regained sovereignty and the brothers were able to create one of the best hotels in Canada.

The old hotel and the grubby, run-down log cabins gradually gave way to a new, one-hundred-room post and beam structure.

Some of the cosiest rooms are log cabin duplexes: living area and riverstone fireplace downstairs, loft bedroom upstairs

The snow! The snow! Lake Louise is probably your best bet for skiing fresh powder snow in all Canada

Rugged yet simple interiors are just what you might expect of a mountain hideaway in the midst of awesome scene

For people wanting more privacy or space, there is also a handful of log cabins scattered about the property

The largest, most comfortable room is this massive two-storey library, complete with bridge tables (and books)

The rugged, no-nonsense architectural style of the Post Hotel is known as 'post and beam'

The Post celebrates the region's heritage in everything down to the smallest detail. Old photos of Lake Louise from the early 1900s decorate the corridors; riverstone fireplaces, slate floors, timber-beamed ceilings and leaded glass set the tone for the spacious guest suites; and in the two-storey library the ambience pays tribute to the Scottish baronial heritage of the former owner.

The restaurant is a major drawcard. The bus driver was right: it *is* one of the best places to eat in western Canada. The service is Italian-style, with an army of very professional white-jacketed European waiters, and the menu is a clever mix of local flavour and international sophistication. Specialities include buffalo filet and pastas prepared with wild mushrooms and truffles. The true measure the Post restaurant is that many dinner guests make the effort to come from the nearby Chateau Lake Louise, itself well-served with fine restaurants. And then of course there's the reason the Schwarz brothers came here in the first place from the Italian-Swiss area of Ticino, namely the skiing. Just five minutes by shuttle from the Post, it has all the bowls, gulleys, trails and steep faces that comprise the complete skiing experience. Your chance of skiing untracked powder is probably greater here than at any other resort in Canada. The scenery is of the postcard variety – craggy peaks, blue sky, frozen white lakes, and sugar-crusted trees. Although there are literally thousands of acres of skiable terrain, Lake Louise is probably most famous for the bowls that run down the back of the mountain. From a summit elevation of 8,650 feet (2,600 metres) they drop 3,000 feet (900 metres) for what even the most conservative ski guides describe as truly steep terrain. And the best news? Lake Louise is predominantly a summer tourism spot. In winter it's relatively quiet, perfect for skiers who don't want to share their mountains with too many others. Whistler Blackcomb in British Columbia may be bigger, but Lake Louise is colder, steeper, quieter and, according to most, prettier.

address The Post Hotel, PO Box 69, Lake Louise, Alberta, Canada, T0L 1E0

t +1 (403) 522 3989 **f** +1 (403) 522 3966 **e** info@posthotel.com

room rates from Cdn $185

breithorn hotel

The best places sometimes come as a complete surprise. I was on my way out of Champoluc, already quite pleased with my discovery of the unspoiled Monterosa ski area, when the old Alpine village's bizarre one-way traffic system led me to stumble upon the Breithorn Hotel.

Vintage prints attest to the fact that well-dressed ladies and gentlemen used to make their way here in the late 1800s to escape the summer heat of Milan and Turin. The area has changed very little since then. The road isn't much wider than it was in those days, and along the way you pass through one farming village after another in which the way of life remains intimately connected to the seasons and the land. Tiny chapels decorated with naive frescoes sit on the vantage points, and here and there crudely constructed weathered log granaries survive, elevated on chiselled mushroom-shaped stones to keep the rats out. Once upon a time, these simple rustic testaments to the agrarian nature of Alpine life were ubiquitous. But ski tourism, particularly in larger resorts, has made them very scarce. Zermatt still has a few granaries, but they are squeezed in between row after row of sports shops, jewellers, and big hotels. To say they are incongruous is an understatement. But around

Champoluc, where farmers still outnumber retailers and development has been minimal, they don't look out of place at all. Champoluc still feels and looks like Alpine hamlets did before the ski boom turned every other villager into a caterer or a ski instructor. Sure the resort of Monterosa gets its share of skiers, but not in the manic unrelenting fashion of, say, Kitzbühel and Verbier. It is to Italy what Ischgl is to Austria: one of the most underrated and overlooked ski areas in the Alps. High, steep, snow-safe and linked to both Cervinia and Zermatt, it is one of the treasures of the Aosta Valley.

Ancient granaries are the reason I first noticed the Breithorn. Initially I didn't know it was a hotel; I stopped because I was fascinated by the texture of this primitive architecture and the orderly fashion in which it had been incorporated into the existing exterior. Somebody had taken a great deal of trouble and care to adapt this ages-old vernacular on the outside of their building; logic dictated that the interior might be similarly attention-grabbing. I was right: roughly hewn granite floors, richly coloured fabrics, oriental rugs, antique furniture, big landscape oil paintings in monumental gilded frames and lots of faded,

textured and thoroughly beaten-up old wood combine to create an ambience both baronial and Alpine. It's just as you might imagine the chalet of a reclusive Italian industrialist to look – full of beautiful things intended for comfort and enjoyment, not for showing off.

What's clever about the Breithorn is that it looks – outside and in – as if it's always been this way, an old gem in an old gem of a town. And that's exactly what it is – almost. The Breithorn is certainly not new. In fact it was the first hotel in the valley, built back in 1903 to cater to summer escapees from Italy's industrial cities. But it didn't always look this way. A century ago it was a big box in a tiny town. Comfort, not cultural consistency, was the original aim of Alpine hospitality, and an aristocratic clientele expected hotels to be as big and grand as possible. Cosy, in their world, was synonymous with small, dirt-poor and uncomfortable – understandable when they had to wear stiff collars, suits, dress shoes and a hat even for breakfast. The dress code for

hotel architecture was equally strict, which explains how the tiny hamlet of Champoluc ended up with a grand six-storey block. It may have been culturally inappropriate, but that thought would not have crossed many minds in those days, when the Italian Alps were still completely untouched. Now that the original built culture of these mountains is threatened with extinction, the Breithorn has opted to reinvent itself in the local vernacular, becoming a rustic fantasy that supplies creature comforts cloaked in local tradition. Eiderdowns, *naif* painted timber cupboards and traditional panelled walls coexist with brand new bathrooms, cable TV and internet portals. Two restaurants, a bar, a brasserie and a spa complex hide behind granite and old wood cladding that once sheltered nothing more than hay bales and grain. It's a formula that works perfectly for the modern skier – all the rugged charm of an old-fashioned Alpine interior without a hint of the rough-edged inconvenience.

address Breithorn Hotel, Route Ramney, 27-11020 Ayas-Champoluc-Valle d'Aosta, Italy
t +39 (0125) 308 734 **f** +39 (0125) 308 398 **e** info@breithornhotel.com
room rates from €72

hotel california

If sleep is not high on your list of priorities, you are going to love Hotel California. As you may have already guessed, this is a music hotel, and all its rooms and suites are dedicated to vinyl legends. There's a Doors room, a Joan Baez room, a Janis Joplin room, a Bob Dylan room, a Marshall Tucker Band room, a Byrds room, and of course a room dedicated to the King. You don't even need to open your eyes to know which one you are in: the music of each dedicated artist begins playing the minute you turn on the lights.

It may sound like a gimmick, but it's not. Every single guest room at Hotel California has been custom-wired with one of the most sophisticated specialized sound systems I have come across. Mounted on each bedhead is a control panel with buttons for volume and track selection. Track number one is always the music the room is dedicated to. Thus if you are in the Doors room, one of my favourites, press track one and you will get 180 minutes of some of the best music the Doors ever recorded. In the Janis Joplin room, track one will get you 180 minutes of Janis live as well as the best tracks from different albums. But you are not limited to the musician of your room's theme, because each individual sound system also

includes 180 minutes of all the other featured artists on tap: just select the number.

One thing is certain: these rooms were put together by a real music lover, and one with a lot of conviction in his own taste. If you can't stand to listen to Crosby, Stills, Nash and Young, the Grateful Dead, the Byrds, the Doors or Dylan, then find another hotel. But if you can get into the music, it's a joy to be able to blast your favourite tracks as loud as you want from a set of really decent speakers. The slave-to-the-music theme dominates throughout. There's a jukebox in the lobby and most of the ground floor is occupied by the kind of bar that gets trashed by musos in road movies.

With long straggly hair and beaten-up leather waistcoat, proprietor Guido even looks like a rock star – a slightly faded one. Hotel California, as he will tell you, didn't start as a hotel. It started as a big hole in the ground. The first thing Guido did – in fact the only thing he did before the money ran out – was to sink a huge concrete foundation. He had grand plans, but the finances just wouldn't allow them, so instead he started a disco. What better way to make use of a concrete bunker? Champoluc's only disco was a big hit.

65

The disco was followed by a small bar, this time above ground. While his wife Marina was working in the bar, Guido was outside building stage three – a pub. This was originally going to be a 150-seat restaurant, but when three other restaurants opened in the village, Guido decided to create Champoluc's first pub instead, probably still the only place in the whole of the Aosta Valley area to serve Guinness on tap. Eventually the restaurant did become a reality too. It was built directly above – in fact hanging over – the saloon-type pub.

The final instalment in the organic expansion of Guido's three-dimensional musical fantasy was the hotel. In design, it is just as eclectic as the rest of the place. Apart from their music posters, the corridors look a little like something out of a Wild West boarding house. The rooms, in complete contrast, are thoroughly contemporary in style, with halogen bedside lamps, trendy telephones, and multi-coloured tiled bathrooms. Guido is very proud of his creation, and so are the

locals, who will all tell you with enthusiasm that this is the best hotel in the area (although a sneaky suspicion tells me that what they really mean is that it's the best hotel to party!). In the middle of winter the place is buzzing, and just as importantly the skiing is among the best – and least known – in the Italian Alps. The tiny town of Champoluc lies at almost 2,000 metres (6,500 feet) and is within skiing distance of two of the Alps' more familiar resorts, Zermatt and Cervinia. For adventure-seekers, there's a heli-skiing option which starts at 4,000 metres (13,000 feet), takes you off-piste all the way to Zermatt and then back via another route to the slopes of Monterosa.

Old rockers, young snowboarders, night owls and party people will surely warm to Hotel California's strange mix of Memphis pop, Irish pub and Alpine night club. If, however, you prefer an early night after your day on the slopes, then be warned. As Guido himself will happily tell you, 'dees ees not a place for tranqueelitee.'

---

address Hotel California, West Road, Ayas (AO), Italy

t +39 (0125) 307 977 **f** +39 (0125) 307 977 **e** info@wrpub.com

room rates from € 67

hotel hermitage

Talk about being spectacularly lost. The people at the Hotel Hermitage in Cervinia, on the Italian side of the Matterhorn, had assured me that it was very much easier to ski there from Zermatt than to drive. By car the journey would take eight hours, on skis just one. I didn't need much convincing. I got a trail map, put the cameras in the backpack, and headed off.

Leaving Zermatt village early, I took the electric bus to the edge of town, followed by a cable car that took me to 2,000 metres (6,500 feet), another that took me to 3,000 metres (10,000 feet) and finally the last cable car, which took me to the peak of the Kleine Matterhorn, little brother to the Matterhorn − though at 4,000 metres-plus (13,000 feet), not exactly a molehill. Indeed it's the highest skiable point in the world outside the Himalayas. To get to the pistes you need first to negotiate what they call the Gletscher Grotto, a dark, foreboding tunnel that takes you to the smoother side of the Matterhorn's craggy peaks. I emerged to find it snowing furiously, a wind blasting across the summit, visibility about ten metres and a temperature of -17°C. It was 8.30 in the morning, I didn't know the mountain, and simply following the red poles planted in the snow, as I had been advised, didn't inspire confidence. So I was very relieved to come across two skiers who were more familiar with the terrain. 'Excuse me, do you know the way to Italy?' I enquired. 'Yes,' they said, 'it's very simple. Just keep going left.' In German it sounded convincingly emphatic: '*Links, links, immer links.*'

They were right. Three quarters of an hour and two kilometres of vertical later, I arrived in Cervinia, the highest village in Italy − though to be frank, not its prettiest. It doesn't have the eco-friendly car-free policy of Zermatt, and nor, at 2,000 metres does it have a pre-skiing history as a farming community. Founded by Mussolini, Cervinia embodies many of the more unappealing sides of modern Italy, and parking is certainly a problem. That said, if you are lucky enough to stay at Hotel Hermitage, my bet is that you won't notice the town because you won't leave the hotel except to ski.

Hotel Hermitage is one of those places that manages to get just about everything right. Situated just behind Cervinia's main cable car, which takes you to the Plateau Rosa at 3,400 metres (11,000 feet), it's in the quietest part of town, among trees, with a stunning view of the

Matterhorn. The building is a handsome and appropriate mix of granite and timber – Alpine in feel but not retro or nostalgic. Its slate-tiled roof and carved timber detailing are recognizably of these mountains, but all is executed in a sober and simple style that shows considerable refinement and taste.

The same is true of the interior. Hermitage's lobby is big, comfortable and filled with light, and its huge fireplace is always burning. La Chandelle restaurant – also with a view of the Matterhorn – is equally spacious, and for once the tables are set far enough apart to mean you don't have to share your neighbour's conversation. The food is in the traditional style of the Aosta Valley – brown farmer's bread, plenty of cheeses and *charcuterie*, and the kind of rich pastas filled with cheese, butter and sage that are so suited to the climate and activity of the mountains. The one style peculiarity is that everything is green: green tablecloths, green napkins, green curtains, green upholstery, and waiters in green jackets. It's certainly not my favourite colour, but it works at the Hermitage because it's so consistent.

Perhaps the most surprising aspect of this hotel is the scale of the rooms. Contrary to established Alpine tradition, the guest spaces at the Hermitage are vast. Many have their own sitting room complete with fireplace, and the suite on the top floor, imaginatively located under the sloping gables of the roof, is so convincingly big that many people when they look at a photograph assume it must be the public salon of the hotel.

In style terms, the key word at Hotel Hermitage is warmth – warm colours, warm materials (plenty of timber and wool) and warm lighting. Together these ingredients conspire to create cosy, comfortable cocoons for guests. That's brilliant news for the laid-back vacationer reluctant to get up at the crack of dawn – but bad news for the red-hot skier who might find it just a little harder to be the first on the lift in the morning.

address Hotel Hermitage, 11021 Cervinia, Italy

t +39 (016) 694 8998 **f** +39 (016) 694 9032 **e** info@hotelhermitage.com

room rates from € 400

hameau albert premier

Every week, every Wednesday, every year for seven years, Pierre Carrier would wake up early – really early – tumble bleary-eyed into his car, and drive and drive and drive in search of the perfect old wooden farmhouse.

Pierre Carrier's family has owned and managed the best hotel in Chamonix for more than a century. The Albert Premier was named in honour of the Belgian monarch who was a regular visitor to this famous town at the foot of Mont Blanc. When Pierre came to take his turn at the helm, he and his wife Martine added another dimension to its success by earning two Michelin stars for its restaurant. Pierre worked in the kitchen while his wife looked after the management of the hotel.

What the faithful guests of the Albert Premier could not have guessed was that their host harboured a great love of modern architecture and design. For years he dreamed of creating a more contemporary addition to the family legacy. It remained a romantic dream until the local authorities expressed interest in developing a sports complex on a vacant piece of land adjacent to his hotel. Threatened with yet more of the nondescript concrete architecture that has already spoiled much of Chamonix, Pierre was galvanized into action. He would develop the site in a more sympathetic fashion: he would find an old farm, transport it here, and create a more rustic and also more funky addition to his hotel.

Easier said than done. It's hard enough these days to find an old farm that hasn't been snapped up as a second-home project by a city couple with two kids, a dog and plenty of cash. It's harder still to find one that can be moved. Hence Pierre's long crusade. But they breed them tough in the mountains – tough and stubborn. As a measure of his persistence, consider that Wednesdays were his only day off. For what must have seemed an eternity, he was either in the kitchen or in his car. But as they say, persistence overcomes resistance… eventually. Sure enough, he found the treasure he was looking for. It was transported to Chamonix piece by wooden piece, and then reconstructed like a giant Lego set with splinters.

But what of his vision of doing something modern? That's where the real twist came. On the outside the farm looks as it always would have, an impressive collection of weathered beams, carved timber balconies, and little picture-perfect windows. Inside, particularly in the guest rooms, all is definitely not as it was. Furniture by Le Corbusier and

Gaetano Pesce in bright reds and vivid yellows sits alongside ultramodern sculptural forged black fireplaces. Peek through gaps in the beams of the bedroom areas and you will see bathrooms in grey granite and green glass. Combined with walls of rough-hewn old beams and timber floors, it's an exotic effect – like a contemporary apartment in Milan dropped into a rustic shack. It's a daring combination – and it works.

But why call it the Hameau Albert Premier? Because that's what it is: a village. The complex houses a restaurant, a health spa, an open living space with fireplace divided by a glass wall from an indoor–outdoor swimming pool, thirty-odd guest rooms and a handful of smaller cabins spread around the property. It seems that on all those Wednesdays out, Pierre couldn't resist buying at least something, even if it wasn't quite his dream farmhouse. If it was old and it could be moved, he bought it – everything from shacks to hay sheds to pigeon coops. Most of these structures have also been turned into accommodation, further adding to the diversity of overnight experience on offer.

The glue that cements this assortment of structures together is the century of hospitality experience to which the Carrier family are heirs. Make no mistake, the Hameau offers luxury on a standard equal to any five-star hotel, but it avoids stuffiness and formality. First and foremost Pierre and Martine are skiers, and their *sportif* attitude is pervasive. On their odd free afternoon or in the few hours of the occasional early morning they don't hesitate to head out to experience what Chamonix is famous for: the world's most challenging and exhilarating skiing. One morning I was out early. It had snowed all night, and the place looked like a skier's idea of a fairy tale. The only other soul around was a guy driving a snow plough, with a big smile on his face. He turned out to be Pierre, whose delight in the new snow cover was as if he had never seen the stuff before. Here, I thought, is a man eager to make up for spending seven years in the car.

address Le Hameau Albert Premier, BP 55, 119, impasse du Montenvers, 74402 Chamonix Mont-Blanc, France

t +33 (4) 5053 0509   **f** +33 (4) 5055 9548   **e** infos@hameaualbert.fr

room rates from € 116

la chapelle d'elisa

France has the best skiing in the world, and Chamonix has the best skiing in France – all guidebooks agree. Speak to skiers in the tiniest town in the Colorado Rockies and if they know one word of French it will be *Chamonix*. Eventually, one day, every serious skier wants to make the pilgrimage to this town at the base of the mighty Mont Blanc.

So what's the big attraction? In a word, adventure. Skiers who learned their art on the gently sloping pastures of Austria or in the French purpose-built resorts are in for a surprise. Chamonix is real mountain skiing. Most of the terrain is wild, the weather even on a perfect sunny day is unpredictable, and the area abounds with the type of cliffs and crevasses that feature in action movies. Skiing here is both risky and exhilarating. Enthusiasts shouldn't be put off by the potential danger, but they should not be complacent either. This is not a place to venture out alone, no matter how competent a skier you are. Because the glacier keeps shifting, even the local guides do not know every crevasse, and on a fresh snow-covered day they can appear – dangerously – to be safely solid.

The most extreme off-piste skiing takes place on Les Grands Montets, a mountain that rises from the nearby village of Argentière. It has few pistes to speak of and the strange twisting gradient makes for uncomfortable cruising. But off-piste, provided you have a guide, the possibilities are almost endless. What's more, Les Grands Montets has a clever system in place to preserve conditions and drastically reduce the number of people on the mountain. The cable car that goes to its 3,275-metre (10,700-foot) peak takes a single carload at a time, and it is not part of the ski pass system. You must buy a supplementary ticket for every journey, and then only with a set reservation. Thus if you buy a ticket for a departure at 1.20pm and you miss it, you cannot simply jump on the next cable at 2pm. It's a slow but effective way of guaranteeing that you practically have the place to yourself. The descent possibilities from the peak are so innumerable that there's little chance you will even catch a glimpse of the skiers who came up in the cable car with you.

The only downside to Les Grands Montets is the fact that if you are staying in Chamonix then you will have to stand in line at the bus stop each morning to catch the shuttle. Staying in Argentière would be more convenient, but the choice is not nearly so varied or extensive.

In fact there is a shortage of hotels in Argentière. That is what prompted Elisa Giacomotti to convert the chapel of her farm into what must be the smallest hotel in the Alps. And it just got smaller. She used to have six rooms – five in the farmhouse and one in the chapel. But recently she decided to limit the accommodation to the chapel only.

Truth is if La Chapelle d'Elisa wasn't ski in, ski out, and it was anywhere other than Argentière, it would not be in this book. However, this little chapel is at the foot of the most exciting ski mountain in the world, and even if at present it can't accommodate more than two or three people at a time, it's an extraordinary hotel in an extraordinary setting. Originally built in 1780, it is now a tiny but very cosy three-level cottage. It still has the vaulted ceilings of its ecclesiastical past, much to the delight of everyone who stays there. The kitchen, living area, dining area and sundeck are on the top floor; there's a spacious timber-panelled bedroom on the ground floor;

and the bathroom is in the chapel's former cellars. But the real pull of La Chapelle is the ambience. Situated on the fringe of a pine forest at the base of these majestic peaks, with sweeping views of the surrounding valley, this is a private domain second to none. You can ski from the very top of Les Grands Montets (if you have the legs) to the door of your chapel, never breaking the magical spell of these mountains.

But do be prepared to reassess your abilities and perception of skiing. Venturing off-piste on Les Grands Montets means being equipped with radar beepers, extendable snow probes and a shovel. It means stopping frequently to chop the surface apart to inspect for avalanche danger. Last time I skied these mountains it was January. There were huge snowfalls every night, and all day long the guides would point out places where they had lost colleagues to avalanches. Therein is one more advantage of Chapelle d'Elisa: it's an appropriate place to say a few prayers before you go out each morning.

---

address La Chapelle d'Elisa, 394, chemin de la Rosière, 74400 Argentière, France

t +33 (4) 5054 0017 **f** +33 (4) 5054 2109 **e** giacomot-helisa-.ski@wanadoo.fr

room rates from € 230

hotel ancora

Newcomers to Cortina might find it difficult to tell Hotel Ancora and Hôtel de la Poste apart. Both are right in the middle of town, on the main shopping street that is the thoroughfare of choice when it comes to the obligatory late-afternoon *passeggiata*. Give or take a few of the shops, this street, lined with grand frescoed facades, still looks as it does in the old photos that hang in Ancora's lobby. Like La Poste, Ancora is a family-owned property – built in 1826, the hotel has been in the same family for more than a hundred years. The cuisine at Ancora is more creative, while that at La Poste is more classic. Ancora's lobby is cosier, with a fireplace and a bar, but La Poste has a terrace that's a firm favourite for hot chocolate first thing in the morning or a drink before lunch. Ancora's guestrooms are more comfortable and more decoratively consistent, but La Poste's rooms – particularly on the fourth floor – are more likely to surprise. Ancora has a Viennese coffeeshop that serves crêpes in a pretty hand-painted conservatory; La Poste has a beautiful old wood-panelled *Stube* that was once the town's post office. Some devotees prefer the style of one over the other, but to my mind there's not much in it. In terms of the authentic Cortina experience, they are interchangeable.

On the inside, Hotel Ancora is part Tirol, part La Scala. The lobby features an old carved wooden ceiling and a very beautiful Tirolean ceramic stove or *Kachel*, while the dining room is all vaulted ceiling, columns, cream-painted Louis XVI chairs and the odd bit of gilding. In any other location, particularly a mountain setting, such overworked styling would be excessive; in Cortina, it is as much part of the scene as the celebrated limestone peaks surrounding the village. That's because Cortina d'Ampezzo is 'Italian to its voluptuous core'. Even the visitors are predominantly Italian. Here it's never a surprise to come across a bit of glitz and glamour, it's what one expects: the polished waiters in black tie, the gilt-edge Ginori china, the substantial collection of antiques, the modern art – Hotel Ancora is all theatre, and the starring role is played by its flamboyant proprietor, Flavia Sartor. Every morning she can be found in her ski suit admonishing guests for not being in theirs. 'Darling, you're not skiing today?' she purrs. 'Shame on you. You're a naughty boy. It's such a byooootifoool day.' Then onto the next guest. The irony is that she gets so caught up in her work that she forgets to go skiing herself. Ms Sartor takes great pride in her hotel and an

active role in almost everything. She uses the salon to exhibit modern art, she decorates all the rooms and at night she returns to the dining room in sultry, shimmering evening dress to make sure her army of professional waiters perform to her high standards. Joan Collins couldn't do it better.

Flavia and Renato Sartor pay a lot of attention to how things look – which is perfectly appropriate considering Cortina's reputation as the most beautifully situated ski resort in the world. The scenery was convincing enough for the Sylvester Stallone movie *Cliffhanger*, set in the Rockies, to be shot in the area just around the town. If still in doubt, then take the Faloria Cable, which leaves from the town centre. The car rushes alarmingly towards a huge imposing wall of solid granite. Just when you think it will hurtle straight into the great snow-dusted face of stone rushing towards you, it rises slightly further and finally dumps its passengers on top of one of the impressive cliffs surrounding the town.

Although the skiing isn't half bad even on purely artificial snow, I couldn't help thinking how extraordinary it must be in a good snow year. Everybody I spoke to was nostalgic: 'if only you were here last year, there was so much snow that we were still skiing in June'. High altitude couloirs, steep pistes that run between vertical rock-faces leading to endless forest trails that in turn lead into large open bowls: such variety is not found in too many ski resorts. And even when there is no snow at all, there's always the shopping. Bulgari, Gucci, Paul & Shark, Prada, a gaggle of antiquarians and a horde of specialists in cashmere, jewelry and sunglasses offer more options than you will find in a lot of major cities. The après-ski activity of choice elsewhere in Europe may be drinking, but in Cortina it's window-shopping. Anyone can join in, provided you avoid the ultimate Cortina *faux pas* – you must never participate in the *passeggiata* in the same clothes that you wore on the slopes.

---

address Hotel Ancora, C. so Italia, 62, 32043 Cortina d'Ampezzo (BL), Italy

t +39 (0436) 3261 **f** +39 (0436) 3265 **e** info@hotelancoracortina.com

room rates from € 230

hôtel de la poste

Trust the Italians to find a place that looks this good. Le Corbusier called Italy's Dolomites the most beautiful architecture in the world. When you first see Cortina d'Ampezzo, it is hard to disagree. The town's incredible setting is enhanced by skiing Italian-style: late start, long lunch, perfect suntan, immaculate grooming (slopes and skiers), mobile phones in the lifts, mobile phones on the slopes, and animated Italian conversation in every sun-drenched mountain hut you come across. Skiing in Cortina is like a frozen version of *La Dolce Vita*. You certainly won't hear herds of ski boots clunking around the restaurant early in the morning. Nor will you find the whole town marching out with skis on shoulders at 8.30am as you would in all the larger resorts in France and the US. Many people come to Cortina to enjoy the mountains without ever skiing. Even for skiers, the pace of life is much slower than in most Alpine resorts. Cortina wouldn't have it any other way. Getting to the slopes without an early morning stroll through the village and a leisurely coffee would be as unthinkable as not having a cigarette at the bottom of every piste. The pace of life is good and slow…even if when they do hit the slopes, the Italians ski like they drive – fast and fearless.

For its sheer visual drama, Cortina has to be one of the world's most breathtakingly beautiful places to ski. Cliffs, crevasses, soaring peaks – whichever direction you look, the view is spellbinding. The town lies in a large open bowl hedged on all sides by pointed peaks. Some are 3,000-plus metres high (9,800 feet), but the bowl is so large they never block the sun. Thus Cortina has more than its share of UV – great for the Italian tan, not so great for the snow, as a vast array of snow-making equipment confirms. Unlike other high-altitude resorts, where the barren treeless terrain offers an endless expanse of downhill potential, the higher you go in Cortina, the craggier it becomes. The pistes lie in crevasses between rocky outcrops. It makes for spectacular, if unsettling, skiing. This is not a destination for the faint-hearted: the black runs are very steep, with little room to manoeuvre, and even the red runs of Cortina would be classified black in most resorts. But for snow-making, it is perfect. Every night the snow guns can be pointed right at these naturally occurring gaps and trails.

Ironically, although it feels so convincingly Italian, it's not such a long time since this bit of Europe wasn't in Italy at all. Until World War II, this was the southernmost part of Austria.

The view from La Poste offers two layers of inspiration – one manmade, the other courtesy of Mother Nature

A cosy, timber-panelled *Stube* survives intact from the days when the hotel was also the town's post office

Skiing in Italy, particularly in Cortina is an emotive combination of dash, cash and *cucina*

The family tradition of hospitality began in 1835, when the hotel became the official stop for the mail coaches

Dominated by a 17th-century tapestry and two monumental chandeliers, the dining room has a touch of La Scala

The pewter collection in the ground floor *Stube* was started by the present proprietor's great-great-grandfather

Unlike the bedrooms, bathrooms tend to be modern and utilitarian – there is nothing unpredictable about them

The old post office is one of the most popular bars to meet at the end of a day's skiing

With its collection of churches and Renaissance buildings, Cortina is one of the most elegant towns in the Alps

More Austrian than Italian, the *Stube* serves as a reminder that this area of Italy used to be part of Austria's Südtirol

Hôtel de la Poste couldn't be more central – a hop, skip and a jump from the cable car and the best shops

Dinner at La Poste is an elegantly theatrical affair served by an army of dinner-jacketed professional waiters

ew skiers would disagree that Cortina probably the most stunningly located ski resort in the world

Cortina lies within a giant bowl surrounded by the craggy 3,000-metre (9,800-foot) peaks of the Dolomites

Quirky and unpredictable, the guestrooms at Hôtel de la Poste are an eclectic ensemble of different sizes and styles

More of the family's pewter collection is displayed within frescoed recesses in the dining room

The Tirolean heritage is evident in the *naif* painted antique furniture that decorates the marble-tiled corridors

Site of the 1956 Winter Olympics, Cortina is just as popular with serious skiers as with serious non-skiers

Still today, in nearby Pustertal (Pusteria), you will find more people speaking German than Italian, as well as the local language, Ladino, a mix of old Latin and German. Gottardo Manaigo, the fifth-generation proprietor of Hôtel de la Poste, was the first member of his family to complete national service in the Italian army. His father served in the Austrian corps, and the family spoke German at home. Unlike Pustertal, however, Cortina *is* thoroughly Italian. The Italian jetset have made it their winter destination. The sister of Gianni Agnelli has a house here, as does the publisher Arnoldo Mondadori. Marcello Mastroianni did his military service in the Dolomites and retained a lifelong affinity for these mountains.

The Tirolean-Italian heritage makes an interesting mix, and Hôtel de la Poste embodies it to perfection. Its wood-panelled lounge or *Stube* that was at one time the post office is a typical Tirolean affair, as are the corridors full of painted wooden antiques. Yet the dining room, with its coffered ceiling, enormous chandeliers and ornate damask-clad chairs, is pure Italy, as is the army of dinner-suited waiters. In the bedrooms, gilded mirrors and padded silk bedheads are combined with peasant furniture. No two rooms are the same. Sometimes the eclectic mix works, sometimes it doesn't. The slightly ungainly lobby furniture contrasts with oriental rugs on the marble floors of the corridor. All in all, it is a mix that is as varied and unpredictable as the guests. The hotel guest book is full of famous names and royal titles, as well as skiers from every continent. Some Italian families have been coming so long they leave their luggage until the next season. There's a sophisticated ease to this hotel that has a lot to do with the fact that it has been run by the same family since 1835, when an earlier Gottardo Manaigo was granted the official right to receive the town's mail and messages. He soon turned over his home to accommodate the travellers who arrived on the mail coaches, and so a great tradition was born.

---

address Hôtel de la Poste, Piazza Roma, 14, 32043 Cortina d'Ampezzo (BL), Italy

t +39 (0436) 4271 **f** +39 (0436) 868 435 **e** posta@hotels.cortina.it

room rates from € 117

hotel planchamp

Planchamp is the perfect little hotel in the perfectly charming little ski resort of Valmorel. But I confess that I hadn't heard of Valmorel until a couple of years ago when I was skiing in Megève with a girl named Capucine. It was a perfect winter's day: plenty of snow, plenty of sun, and a rendez-vous at L'Alpage du Pré Rosset to take some photographs. The two-hour journey there takes you up most of the ski lifts of Rochebrune, L'Alpette, and Côte 2000. It's a great adventure enhanced by great scenery, but all along the way Capucine just couldn't stop comparing it to Valmorel. 'What a beautiful day!' I exclaimed. 'Yes,' came the tentative response, 'but Valmorel is so much more beautiful.' 'Isn't the snow great?' 'I guess so…but the snow at Valmorel would be better today.' 'But what about the skiing? I know, let me guess, it would be better in Valmorel….'

By the end of the day I had heard more than enough about Valmorel. But I admit my curiosity was piqued. If this place was so great, why hadn't I heard of it, and for that matter, where was it? It had me intrigued – I thought I knew most of the ski resorts in France. I had to go, if only to see for myself if it lived up to the billing.

Valmorel, it turns out, is en route to Les Trois Vallées, but blink and you will miss the turn-off. Like many mountain towns in France, it was purpose-built for skiing, but unlike giant eyesores such as La Plagne or Haute Tignes, this is a place where the property developers did their best to prescribe an architecture that looks like it belongs. Today the village appears small, rustic and low-key, like some places in Austria and Switzerland, and a large underground car park built into the mountain (shades of Saas-Fee) hides most of the cars.

Valmorel is generally billed as a family resort, but Capucine was right: the skiing can be a lot more challenging than those words would imply. The whole area – with 56 lifts and 152km (95 miles) of pistes – is known as Le Grand Domaine, and it connects to the resorts of St François and Longchamp in the Maurienne Valley. Considering that this valley is now also accessible via the massive Trois Vallées lift network, it's conceivable that you could start in Valmorel and ski all the way to Val Thorens. Even without such recently expanded possibilities, Valmorel can be surprisingly rewarding, particularly off-piste. Given its reputation as a family resort,

Moody, dark and full of character, Planchamp offers traditional Savoyard style at unusually affordable prices

Old skis, new resort – Valmorel is one of the most attractive purpose-built French ski resorts

This downstairs area is one of three different dining options at Planchamp and one of Valmorel's finest restaurant

Looking at the vaulted bar, it's hard to believe that this hotel is not an authentically historic fixture

The Planchamp guestrooms are clad entirely in timber. Texture and ambience make up for lack of space

A vaulted bar, a salon with open fire, two restaurants and enough old timber to satisfy the most sceptical traditionalist

it is not exactly prominent on the average powder hound's hit list – which is precisely why the snow stays untracked for longer. In any case, the 'family' reputation of the resort says more about its facilities and services than the challenges – or limitations – of the skiing. Valmorel is without doubt one of the best places in the French Alps to learn to ski. It has separate enclosed training areas for adults and children. No snowboards are allowed on these particular slopes, and nor are more confident skiers en route elsewhere. The resort also has one of the Alps' best mountain nurseries, called the Saperlipopette. With a ratio of no more than five children per nanny, there's a good chance that their skiing will improve more than yours.

At the end of the day there is the car-free heart of Valmorel to return to, known as Bourgmorel. Planchamp is bang in the middle of this small and unassuming village. Even so, you will almost certainly walk straight past the entrance, so subtle is the signage outside.

Once inside, the style is warm and cosy, with an authentic Savoyard flavour. Vaulted ceilings, panelled walls, antique skis, welcoming open fires, rustic furniture, vintage photos, masses of red-and-white gingham check, hand-embroidered cushions – it's hardly an original look, but it is perfectly appropriate in the French Alps, particularly a cosy little destination like Valmorel.

Where Planchamp does differ from other places that have gone the traditional route is that it is surprisingly affordable – cheap, even, by Alpine standards. It's clear that proprietor Jean-Pierre Chevallier and his wife envisaged a place in step with Valmorel itself, in every respect. The town has neither the shopping nor the cosmopolitan buzz of places like Courchevel, Megève, Zermatt or St Moritz, but nor does it pretend to. It doesn't aspire to sophistication, it aspires to deliver enjoyment of the mountains in an honest, hospitable, cosy and – most importantly – affordable manner.

address Hotel Planchamp, 73260 Valmorel, France

t +33 (4) 7909 9700 **f** +33 (4) 7909 8393 **e** info@hotelplanchamp.com

room rates from €93

le mélézin

This was Europe's first Aman. As Adrian Zecha, creator and chairman of the very successful and very exclusive Aman hotel group will tell you, there's no magic formula – he just creates the kind of places he'd like to stay in himself. Since he's a skier, it was perhaps only a matter of time before he opened an Aman ski resort. And Courchevel 1850 was an entirely predictable location. But the architecture and design are quite another story. I didn't get it at first, I admit. The typical low-key Aman approach was familiar, as was the sotto voce discretion of the staff. But usually I can look at the work of Paris-based architect Ed Tuttle and the cultural link with the location is easily evident. Perhaps I was expecting a pared-down version of the classic old wooden farmhouse of Savoie heritage. Le Mélézin is nothing like that. It has no old wood, no splintered beams, no stone floor, no old clocks, no farm tools, no antlers, no rustic anything.

In design terms this was a bold move. Take away every visual cliché of the mountains, and what have you got left? Nothing predictable, that's for sure. At first it's all a bit of a shock. If it doesn't feel and look like a ski hotel, will it still feel like a ski vacation? The answer is a resounding yes. Spaces are cosy, but in an

urbane way – a manner that is more modern, less mountain man. Colours are dark and handsome, textures range from the oiled beauty of exotic timber to parched leather, silver mirror and linen carpet. They are very beautiful, but they are not the elements of a mountain culture – or so I thought.

But there is a reference to the historic Savoie. Stand back from Le Mélézin – quite a way back – and you start to see it in the shape of the building. It looks like the fortified castles found at strategic points throughout the Alps. In some areas they are now nothing more than broken shells; in others, such as along Lac d'Annecy, they are still inhabited. Suddenly, dark oak chairs with elaborately turned legs and brass-studded seats don't seem so improbable. They are what the local baron would have had in his castle. The oak panelling inset with parchment leather, the fruit motif on the embroidered cushions, the silver-mirrored panels and the deep dark colours all derive from an imaginative interpretation of a late-medieval fortress. Yet in no way does this feel like a historic interior. The history is as inspiration, not imitation. What's more, the dominant ambience of Le Mélézin has something decidedly Asian about it.

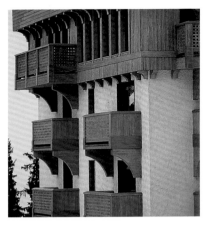

The architecture of Le Mélézin is inspired by the distinctive hilltop forts and castles of the Savoie

Surrounded by pine trees, Le Mélézin's guest rooms are particularly private – no other hotels to look out on and vice versa

In typical Aman fashion, the bedrooms are huge, with big glass doors letting in plenty of light

Here and there, the aesthetic of Le Mélézin is distinctly Asian – a reference to the Aman origins

The terrace adjoining the ski slopes is a popular place to stop for hot chocolate in ski boots

The odd nod to Alpine convention comes in small isolated instances, such as this collection of old wooden tools

Le Mélézin's combination of European simplicity, Asian touches and Alpine texture was the creation of Ed Tuttle

Dining at Le Mélézin is an elegant affair: white linen, velvet upholstery, lots of silver and a calm, subdued atmosphere

Frette linen, quilted bedspreads, a panelled headboard: attention to detail is a reliable Aman signature

Black leather on baronial chairs, oiled timbers and gilded light fittings set the distinctly aristocratic decorative tone

Granite floors in various shades and bleached-wooden chairs offer a pared-down take on mountain materials

Situated above the village of Courchevel 1850, Le Mélézin's main salon looks over the nearby lifts and pistes

Sitting on the edge of one of Courchevel's pistes, Le Mélézin is a genuine ski in, ski out hotel

The upper-floor suites are like elegant apartments, with high coffered ceilings, fireplaces and separate living room

As with most Amans, Le Mélézin has a library. This one is a large, laid-back space on the lower ground floor

e Mélézin looks and feels like no other ski hotel: a neo-baronial hangout on Courchevel's fashionable slopes

A spectacular hammam fashioned from pale French limestone is the star feature of the hotel's health spa

Dark and elaborately turned timber chairs with brass buttoning belong to the hilltop *Schloss* heritage of the Savoie

This flavour comes not from the materials and ingredients but from the overriding calm. The staff, despite being European, are unflappable. Even a small contingent of Russian businessmen pacing the main lobby on their mobile phones yelling '*Da, Da, Nyet, Nyet, Dollaar, Dollaar*' didn't faze anyone. Normally ski hotels are a cacophony of clunking boots, squealing children and checklisting mothers. At Le Mélézin, the loudest noise in the morning is the waiter rolling the well-stocked breakfast trolley to the next table. There's no John Cleese-type hotelier running around telling everyone to shut up. The calm is self-imposed. It quite simply feels like the most appropriate demeanour in the surroundings, and it proves what architects have been telling us for some time: design can introduce a sense of calm, an atmosphere of peace and relaxation. If the return bookings at Le Mélézin are anything to go by, it's a big hit with the clientele. Seldom have I been in a place where the customers are so eager to

rebook. Apparently more than sixty per cent of Le Mélézin's reservations are the result of customers seeking to duplicate the experience – same room, same week, same hotel. It makes it a lot more difficult to get a booking in the first place, though for Le Mélézin it's a good problem to have.

With a world-class hammam, a thoroughly equipped spa that offers the finest Oriental treatments, and a new indoor pool, Le Mélézin is the serene alternative to the 'ski-all-day, drink-all-night, collapse-in-a-heap' ski break. It's a soothing and secure environment. The year before last I had somehow misplaced my ski boots and spent a fruitless twelve months searching for them. On my second visit to Le Mélézin, it dawned on me that perhaps I had left them here. I had long since given up on them, but I mentioned it to the staff all the same. Fifteen minutes later they emerged with my boots, which I had left in the boot room one year earlier. Imagine that in a revolving-door, check-them-in, chuck-them-out ski hotel.

address Le Mélézin, Rue de Bellecôte, 73120 Courchevel 1850, France

t +33 (4) 7908 0133   **f** +33 (4) 7908 0896   **e** lemelezin@amanresorts.com

room rates from € 500

le st joseph

Of all the ski areas in France, Courchevel tops the list in property prices. It's dearer than Chamonix and even Megève. This has a lot to do with choice, for Les Trois Vallées is the largest linked ski resort in the world. But Courchevel property prices also have to do with global warming. At a time when many ski guidebooks start with dire warnings of the devastating effects of increased temperatures in the Alps, being a snow-safe resort gains value all the time.

According to the United Nations' panel on climate change, the Alps are heating up faster than any other region. It's quite possible that the snow line – at present an average altitude of 1,200 metres (4,000 feet) – could shift to 1,800 metres (6,000 feet). Unheard-of temperatures are occurring at altitudes that previously have only recorded minus degrees. My own experience supports the statistics. Last year for example it was plus five degrees at the top of Les Grands Montets in February, an altitude of 3,400 metres (11,000 feet). Since 1850, European glaciers have lost a third of their surface area and more than half their volume. Aside from being bad news for low-lying resorts such as Kitzbühel, Grindelwald and Gstaad, this Alpine warming is also

endangering the permafrost, the perpetually frozen ground above 2,500 metres (8,200 feet). Because permafrost does not support significant vegetation, it is prone to devastating mudslides if it thaws. There is also the danger that the massive pylons anchoring ski lifts could start to shift – an engineering and safety nightmare. Thus today it is no longer possible to rate a resort on grounds of charm and authenticity alone; today it's also very much about altitude.

At 1,850 metres (6,000 feet) the village of Courchevel 1850 is well and truly snow-safe. Indeed its altitude ensures a season that can be enjoyed well into April and usually starts a month before Christmas. The lift system of the enormous Trois Vallées ski area is the most efficient on the planet. And the biggest in the world just got bigger, with a fourth valley – the Maurienne – being added by way of a new high-speed gondola. Les Trois Vallées – now Les Quatre Vallées – has a huge network of over two hundred chairs, gondolas and cable cars, all high-speed. They link what is conservatively estimated at 600 km (380 miles) of groomed pistes and countless more of off-piste terrain. Even if you were to stay all winter it's doubtful you could ski all the slopes. And therein lies another major attraction. If, like most people, your skiing is limited to a couple of weeks each winter, then Courchevel is a place you can return year after year and still have a new adventure each time. The Parisians certainly do – one more reason why the real estate is the most expensive in the French Alps.

Courchevel is a purpose-built resort, but probably the most charming of its kind in France. It's not a real town of course – such altitude was prohibitive for traditional farmers – but compared to the likes of Risoul, Les Arcs, La Plagne and Flaine, it is conspicuously upmarket. Courchevel tries hard to recreate the rustic charm that comes naturally to lower villages in the Savoie, and not without success, even if its charming bits are interspersed with messy property developers' mistakes.

Le St Joseph is an honest attempt to reclaim the seductive signature of the real Savoie. In a town that counts more four- and five-star hotels than any other in France except Paris, Le St Joseph is one of the first to take the traditional route in style and ambience.

Courchevel, like Megève, certainly has its share of people who do nothing more *sportif* than arranging where to have lunch. But the brand of authentic mountain charm that Megève does so well has been slow coming to Courchevel. Until recently the predominant style of hotels here was more St Tropez than St Bernard. Courchevel even has a winter counterpart to St Tropez's famous Hotel Byblos – though its attempt to get funky with exaggerated use of neoclassical icons is not so successful in the snow as it is on the beach.

The idea of St Joseph was to plant an old-fashioned hotel in Courchevel – and to do it so convincingly that it looks and feels like it has always been here. That required sumptuous old-fashioned decor, old-fashioned service and old-fashioned comfort. Using real antiques and Savoyard touches, the illusion of age has been so successfully achieved that many an American guest is disappointed to discover the truth. Perhaps the only thing missing from the formula is some good old-fashioned lying.

---

address Le Saint Joseph, Rue Park City, 73120 Courchevel 1850, France

t +33 (4) 7908 1616 **f** +33 (4) 7908 3838 **e** info@lesaintjoseph.com

room rates from € 360

amangani

The possibilities for scaring yourself are endless. That's the British Ski Club's frank assessment of Jackson Hole's advanced terrain. This collection of chutes, bowls, gulleys and couloirs on the jagged peaks of the Grand Teton ranges in Wyoming makes up the most challenging ski resort in North America. Jackson's steepness and sheer vertical – until recently the longest continuous piste in North America (now overtaken in the statistics department by Aspen's Snowmass) – are legendary. Yet this remote corner of Wyoming has a lot more to offer than skiing. Years before Alpine sport was introduced to the USA, Jackson Hole was famed for its abundant natural beauty. John D. Rockefeller Jr was awestruck by the majesty of the jagged snow-capped Tetons rising massively from the valley floor. Elk roamed in migrating masses (and still do) and every species of American wildlife was to be found. Rockefeller Jr was a philanthropist on a scale almost unimaginable today, committed to using his family fortune to enhance America's heritage. He set about acquiring massive tracts of land in and around Jackson, and then donated them to the people of the United States in the form of a national park. Where Rockefeller went, other wealthy industrialists followed, and in time

Jackson Hole became a place of super-rich but decidedly low-key ranchers.

The old cattle town of Jackson is protected by national wilderness status, and in winter it's not unusual to find the odd elk roaming between the clapboard houses on its main street. And unlike other North American ski resorts, winter not summer is low season. Jackson Hole is the gateway to Yellowstone national park and in summer more than two million visitors, mostly in mobile homes, squeeze through en route to the park and its famous geysers. But in winter, quiet returns and only the skiers arrive to test themselves on famous Rendezvous Mountain.

Given the brute spectacle of its scenery, the charm of its authentic cattle town, and the sterling status of its real estate, it's not so surprising that Jackson Hole became the venue for North America's first Aman resort. Aman, primarily identified with awe-inspiring properties throughout Asia, has developed a bit of a cult following over the past decade. It's fair to say that most Aman junkies were surprised by this choice of venue in the USA. It isn't hot (or even warm), there are no beaches, and these days it doesn't really figure in most people's idea of a dream escape.

But on closer inspection, Jackson Hole was not only an inspired choice, it was quite a characteristic one. Amans are all built in spectacular positions, and Amangani is no exception. Situated on a ridge just outside the old gunslinging town of Jackson, Amangani directly faces the most impressive aspect of the Tetons. The views, mesmerizing in their majesty, are not limited to the odd corner room or well-positioned public space. Every room, every bathroom, every balcony, the health club, restaurant, and even the heated outdoor swimming pool enjoy the same spectacle.

In responding to the extraordinary beauty of the setting, Ed Tuttle – architect of Bali's Amankila and Phuket's Amanpuri – has created a masterpiece of American modernism, rugged yet refined, simple yet sophisticated. If Frank Lloyd Wright had been a skier he would have been first to check in. The long horizontal lines and drystack Oklahoma sandstone construction take the vernacular of a western ranch and serve it up on a monumental scale. It looks completely at home in this wilderness, yet it avoids the most obvious icons of the American west. Instead it makes reference to the untamed splendour of its surroundings in a chic, abstracted manner. The cushions, for instance, are covered in faux bear fur. Chairs are made from the raw woven chamois leather traditionally favoured by Native Americans, but were manufactured specially for Amangani in Asia. Even what look at first sight to be Native American artifacts turn out to be works of contemporary art in materials as unexpected as newsprint. But the single most impressive aspect of the interior is its scale. Vast spaces, towering panes of glass, enormous halls, and grand stairways are contained in a structure that, despite its horizontality, is of proportions normally encountered only in public buildings. In Amangani, Jackson Hole has a hotel in step with the aura of the place. Jackson itself feels, big, open and ruggedly beautiful – just what you imagine the American West to be. Exactly the same can be said for Amangani.

---

address Amangani, 1535 North East Butte Road, Jackson Hole, Wyoming 83001, USA

t +1 (307) 734 7333 **f** +1 (307) 734 7332 **e** amangani@amanresorts.com

room rates from US $700

chesa grischuna

The Chesa is not the largest or the newest or the most luxurious hotel in Klosters, but it is the best. What makes it so special is difficult to pin down – perhaps it's the fact that it has changed so little. By chance I was seated next to a charming elderly couple at dinner. We started talking about the hotel – or rather, they quizzed me to find out what I thought of *their* hotel. They were not the owners, but when guests have returned every winter since the hotel opened in 1938, one can understand their sense of proprietorship.

Chesa Grischuna, on the Bahnhofstrasse in Klosters, is still owned and run by the descendants of Herr Guler, its founder. It's unusual to find a Bahnhofstrasse in a small mountain town, but you can rely on the Swiss to be literal. Klosters's *Bahnhof* – the train station – is a stone's throw from the hotel. Better still, just behind it is the main cable car that takes you to the Gotschna peak. Thus the Chesa couldn't be better situated. The building itself is a handsome piece of traditional Swiss mountain architecture, so it comes as a bit of a surprise that it was conceived, from scratch, by an architect named Hermann Schneider just before World War II. It's obvious that he was a skier, because the entire building oozes the

ambience of the mountains. At lunch there's no objection if you arrive fresh from the slopes in your ski boots (the dark timber floor won't show the dents or the dirt anyway) and all day long guests and non-guests wander in for a hot chocolate, a morning coffee with the papers, or a fast pasta and a glass of wine. There's a wonderfully casual atmosphere, and yet at the same time the Chesa runs like a Swiss clock. From the little basket of delicious petits fours from the local bakery on the reception desk or the homemade Bircher-Muesli at breakfast to the surprisingly cool live entertainment in the vaulted cellar bar downstairs, everything is finely tuned for the guests' enjoyment.

Despite resistance to change, the Chesa is not stuffy or old-fashioned. The food, for instance, is the responsibility of a head chef who is still in his twenties, and who brings a fresh modern approach to traditional mountain fare. You are advised to stick with the menu in the evening because otherwise you might miss out on creative starters like a watercress salad served with a piece of pan-fried fois gras followed by a cream of mushroom Riesling soup and a main course of grilled turbot served on a bed of julienned vegetables splashed with a touch of lime.

The homebaked cinnamon apple and caramel tart may be traditional, but the basil-flavoured ice cream certainly isn't.

With a twinkle in their eyes, my friends at dinner recalled the days when Orson Welles, Cary Grant, Audrey Hepburn and Yul Brynner were regular guests, and when Gene Kelly would entertain them all by dancing on the tables in the Chesa Bar. It's true the movie stars are gone, but time has been kind to the Chesa and to the village of Klosters. The Chesa's style and *Gemütlichkeit* are just what one expects of a chalet. Klosters is still beautiful and, just as important, still *ruhig* or quiet. The community has its fair share of farms and farmers, and in fact quite a few ski instructors round out the day by hand-milking the cows on family farms. Sure, they could sell their land for a fortune – but where would they go? There aren't many places on this planet that can compete with the charm and beauty of Klosters.

That said, I had never skied in Klosters before. All I knew of its slopes was some news footage I once caught of Prince Charles skiing with his two sons. I'm glad to say that Klosters is definitely more exciting than the British royal family make it look. This is what they call a *Riesengebiet*, a giant area where you can ski from Klosters to Davos to Arosa or if you are really adventurous to the Alberg of Austria, ending up in St Anton – the only downside being that you have to go back by bus. Besides the scope and the extent of skiing in Klosters, the other big plus is the grooming. I told my guide: 'no moguls – my knees aren't up to it.' She laughed: 'You won't find any bumps on these mountains.' That's what makes Klosters perfect for intermediate skiers – there are no nasty surprises to ruin your confidence. That plus good old Swiss technology: it's comforting to see a substantial building perched at the very peak of the Klosters ski area with the impressive title Institute for Avalanche Research. No ice, no moguls, no avalanches – no wonder the British royal family won't ski anywhere else.

address Chesa Grischuna Romantik Hotel, Bahnhofstrasse 12, 7250 Klosters, Switzerland
t +41 (81) 422 2222 **f** +41 (81) 422 2225 **e** chesagrischuna@bluewin.ch
room rates from SFr250

riders palace

'Flims is crap.' That's one of the slogans of the Laax-Flims tourist office. Small wonder, you might think, that the area hasn't had more success outside the German-Swiss market. Crap is the rather unfortunate local term for peak, as in mountain peak. But it's inconceivable that the language-savvy Swiss should have committed such an obvious *faux pas*; more likely they decided to make tongue-in-cheek capital out of this potentially awkward term. It makes perfect sense when you learn that Laax-Flims has become one of *the* board-riding destinations in the Alps. With no less than three half-pipes that feature walls of a world-beating 6.7 metres (22 feet) in height, this is a surfer's hotspot that hosts a number of big international snowboarding events. And with such a rider's reputation, places like No Name Café or the Crap Bar should come as no surprise.

Riders Palace opened in 2001 with the same young, unconventional market in mind. The Palace is a cutting-edge contemporary building with the kind of interior spaces normally found in trendy urban locations. In terms of architectural direction, it has more in common with the razor-sharp technology of Oakley sunglasses than the baggy pants and mandatory bit of facial hair that constitute the boarder stereotype. In truth, snowboards have outgrown the grungy skateboard image and snowboarding has attained the status of a mainstream winter sport. It is no longer possible to make assumptions about riders – apart, that is, from their youthful attitude and healthy disregard for convention. Boarders, like hi-tech skiers, are prone to give nostalgia and tradition a miss, and are generally not looking for the Heidi hideaways.

The Riders Palace didn't use to be a palace at all. It was a hostel for backpacking snowboarders and skiers. But the successful development of the area as a snowsurfers' paradise allowed the metamorphosis of the hostel into a tailor-made hi-tech home for free-riding snow enthusiasts. Like the Hotel Pelirocco in Brighton, it went down the corporate sponsorship route. Sony is one of the sponsors, so there are PlayStations and DVD-cinema in the lobby, and some rooms offer a complete multimedia experience, while London's Ministry of Sound runs the nightclub. The slogan of the Palace could be 'shred all day, rave all night, wake up in a pristine room'.

That's why the developers were comfortable to pursue a completely new direction (at least for the snow). At first sight the mirror-glazed

127

facade may seem a bit out of place, but when you consider that all it does is reflect the mountains back at you, it comes to seem a far more attractive approach than the big-white-block sanatorium architecture that used to prevail in Swiss resorts. Inside, the spaces pay homage to the setting. Guestrooms are pure white with the odd splash of colour – not unlike a boarder coming down a pristine empty piste. And speaking of empty, this is one of the resort's greatest drawcards. During the week you can expect to find no queues in the Laax-Flims area. This is one of the most underrated and overlooked resorts of the Swiss mountains, and the most democratic. They could have called this the People's Palace because despite the cutting-edge architecture and ultra-groovy interiors it still caters to the monetarily challenged. Budget boarders can get budget boarding in the same venue – just book a bunk instead of a room.

Riders Palace may be ultra-contemporary, but Laax by and large is old and traditional.

The oldest farmhouse in the tiny hamlet dates back to 1615 and although Laax does not have the chocolate-box appeal of Zermatt or Saas-Fee, it has nonetheless retained the charm of an old farming community. In terms of the skiing, the runs are long and the terrain varied. From the top of La Siala a steep run goes all the way to the village – 1,700 metres (5,600 feet) of pure vertical. The terrain is ideal for adventurous intermediates, and the scenery is some of the best in the Swiss Alps. Like Arosa, Davos and Klosters, it's also quite close to the historic city of Chur, which makes it easy to access some alternative night-time action for those prone to small-village cabin fever.

I've lost count of the number of times I've been to Chur and driven by the sign for Flims – the one with the little skier underneath. 'Flims?' I would think to myself. 'Who on earth would ski in a place called Flims?' Moral of the story: never judge a ski resort, particularly a Swiss one, by its name. Flims is not crap at all.

---

address Riders Palace, CH-7032 Laax, Switzerland

t +41 (81) 927 9700 **f** +41 (81) 927 9701 **e** riderspalace@weissearena.ch

room rates from € 40

lake placid lodge

Lake Placid is better known for the 1980 Winter Olympics than as a ski resort in its own right. The defeat of the Soviet ice hockey team by a bunch of college kids – the so-called 'Miracle on Ice' – produced national euphoria, as did US speedskater Eric Heiden's record-breaking five gold medals. Yet Lake Placid resort, nestled around a stunningly beautiful lake in the shadow of the mighty Whiteface Mountain, remains the best-kept skiing secret on America's East Coast. Skiers from New York, Boston, Albany and even Montreal all flock to the slopes of Vermont, but the fact is that Whiteface is the tallest mountain east of the Mississippi; the vertical at Lake Placid is only just short of that of Aspen and Telluride.

This little town, 160 miles (400 km) south of Montreal, is in the midst of one of the most impressive pieces of wilderness in the United States. At six million acres, the Adirondack Park is bigger than Yellowstone, Grand Canyon and Yosemite combined. It has forty-six mountains over 4,000 feet (1,200 metres) tall, 32,000 miles (50,000 km) of river, 2,000 lakes and ponds, and most is the sole preserve of mountain lions, bears, wolves and moose. After the Iroquois and Algonquin Indians, European trappers came here, drawn by the wild beaver

and mink of these unknown northern woods. And after the trappers came pioneers, farmers from Vermont who ventured across what was then the western frontier. The only resource these hearty folks had in abundance was trees. With axes they fashioned their rough-hewn cabins and furniture – and thus, according to local legend, was born the Adirondack style. By the turn of the twentieth century, the rustic simplicity of this style had been romanticized by the wealthy elites of New York. Every name that has since become an institution in America – Vanderbilt, Carnegie, Rockefeller – built a lakeside retreat in the Adirondacks. Whiteface Mountain, in fact, so reminded the Vanderbilt family of Mount Fuji that they hired Japanese workers to 'Japanize' their camp, and even dressed their maids in kimonos.

'Great camps', as these log extravaganzas were called, were summer destinations – places to escape the intense heat of New York City in August. Their wealthy owners came north to 'rough it' in the wilds – but not without trainloads of nannies, footmen, champagne and silver. So popular were these lakes and mountains, according to author William Murray, that one New Yorker who tried to get into a Saranac Lake hotel in the 1890s found

them all so crowded that he ended up sleeping on the billiard table. Next morning, he was handed a bill of one dollar for each hour he had slept – the rate for playing billiards.

The beauty of winter in this spectacular land was not widely appreciated until 1904 when skiing and ice skating were first offered by the Lake Placid Club – in effect introducing winter sports to the US. Even today, Lake Placid is chiefly thought of as a summer destination… which is all the better for the serious skiers, especially those enjoying the extraordinary setting of the Lake Placid Lodge, where from almost any vista Whiteface Mountain is perfectly in view, flanked by the milky expanse of the frozen lake. The lodge began life in 1882 as Schroeder Camp. In 1896, it was expanded and renamed Camp Coosa. It was operated as a hotel and restaurant for the next century, with different families managing for decades at a time. People came for the natural beauty of the area; in those days the lodge and its cabins were – to be kind – basic. It wasn't until David

and Christie Garrett bought the place in 1993 that it acquired an interior to keep pace with the setting. The Garretts had already achieved tremendous success with their renovation of The Point, on Saranac Lake, and they brought that experience to their new project.

In a word, Lake Placid Lodge is cosy: interestingly and eccentrically cosy. In addition to antiques, oriental rugs and old sepia photos of the lake, all rooms have huge riverstone fireplaces, white birch bark ceilings and coffee tables made of slabs of polished tree trunk. The furniture gives a whole new meaning to the creative possibilities of sticks and twigs. The interiors successfully recreate the Adirondack style of the past, but it feels appropriate rather than nostalgic, and it suits the location to perfection. As Henry David Thoreau said: 'We need the tonic of wilderness. This curious world we inhabit is more wonderful than it is convenient, more beautiful than it is useful. It is more to be admired and enjoyed than used. In wilderness is the preservation of the world.'

---

address Lake Placid Lodge, Whiteface Inn Road, PO Box 550, Lake Placid, NY 12946, USA

t +1 (518) 523 2700 **f** +1 (518) 523 1124 **e** info@lakeplacidlodge.com

room rates from US $350

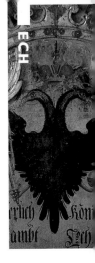

gasthof post

For lovers of traditional Austria, Gasthof Post in Lech is hard to beat. The Arlberg, which also includes the towns of St Christoph, St Anton, Stuben and Zürs, is the best known and most impressive part of the Austrian Alps. Although not as high as comparable resorts in France or Switzerland, its skiable area is nonetheless immense, and the average snowfall is the best in the whole of the Alps. For over a hundred years, mountain enthusiasts have been making the trek through the Arlberg Pass in order to savour the classic traditions of Austria: the *Lederhosen*, the *Loden* hunting jackets, the peaked and feathered caps, the yodelling.

The family-owned Gasthof Post, with its simple carved wooden furniture, its painted fresco decoration, and its owners' adherence to the old ways, fulfils all expectations of Austrian tradition. Frau Moosbrugger, the proprietor, still finds time to embroider every cushion that adorns the dining room, complete with the date of her handiwork. Some mornings, you will find manager Florian in his ski pants, having been up the mountains before reporting for duty. Every antler on the wood-panelled walls is labelled with the date and place of where the creature was shot – no off-the-shelf antlers here, one suspects.

Despite all this, Gasthof Post is no longer the old timber structure that Florian's grandfather purchased in 1937. In those days all the Moosbruggers could offer was running water, a three-hundred-year-old farmhouse parlour, a collection of stables, pigsties, sheep pens and chicken houses, and a bunch of horsedrawn sleighs out front for picking up guests at the railway station in Langen. Electricity didn't arrive in Lech until 1924 and access by road for cars was not completed until 1950. Thirty-five years on, in 1972, a second generation of Moosbruggers responded to the tourism boom by deciding to demolish and build anew. The original hotel doesn't exist at all any more. Certain details, such as doors and an ornate wood-panelled ceiling, were salvaged, but otherwise the present hotel is all new. The Moosbruggers reasoned that the loss of character would be compensated by greater luxury and space. They were right, and what's more, despite all the luxury, Gasthof Post remains very much a ski hotel: the ski room has a repair station; guests put on their boots seated on a traditional ceramic *Kachel*; tea, cakes and hot chocolate are served in the library when you return from the piste; and most guests arrive for breakfast in ski gear.

More important is that the ambience of tradition has been preserved. Guests get their luxuries – big bathrooms, powerful showers, double sinks, state-of-the-art communications – while the interiors remain everything one would expect from an Austrian Gasthof.

One of the most attractive aspects of skiing in Austria's Vorarlberg is the fact that its resorts have evolved rather than been created. Towns and villages are working communities as well as holiday destinations, and Vorarlbergers have fun with you rather than simply profiting from your fun. It's this genuine interaction that creates great loyalty – that and the fact that the best Austrian *Gasthäuser* are almost always a family affair. And in terms of either guest loyalty or family tradition, there can be few places more impressive than Gasthof Post. In a book published to celebrate the Post's sixty-year jubilee, there is a list of the most loyal guests over the years. There are plenty of famous names, but even more impressive are the categories the list is divided into. There are the diamond guests, who have been coming on a regular basis for 45 years, the sapphire group 35 years, the ruby 25 years, gold 18 years, and silver a measly 10 years. Among the most loyal Post guests are the Dutch royal family, who have been spending winter vacations here since 1960. Their different generations feature in almost every list, which is all the more remarkable considering that with the family shareholding wealth in Shell they could easily afford their own pad in the Alps. Instead Queen Beatrix and clan choose to remain loyal to the Post, where over the decades they have become close friends with the Moosbruggers.

The loyalty is reciprocal. The Shah of Iran had heard about the famous Gasthof Post, but he couldn't get a room because it would have meant turning away regulars. Princess Grace and Prince Rainier also left it too late to book. The Moosbruggers are refreshingly matter-of-fact when dealing with royals. As they say, 'in Lech no one notices a princess in the lift queue – in anorak and sunglasses we're all the same.'

address Gasthof Post, Lech 11, A-6764 Lech-am-Arlberg, Austria

t +43 (5583) 220 60 **f** +43 (5583) 220 623 **e** info@postlech.com

room rates from € 200

au coin du feu

Poor little Megève. Ever since Baroness Noémie de Rothschild took the advice in 1916 of her Norwegian ski instructor to create a French version of St Moritz out of this tiny Haute Savoie village, it's been branded the fur coat capital of the French Alps. And these days, that's not a compliment. Mention Megève to skiers and most will immediately dismiss it as too *chichi*, with lousy skiing. Then ask if they've ever been there and they will reply rather sheepishly that they haven't. It's just what they have heard or read.

The old adage still applies: throw enough mud and some will stick. Megève has an image problem − mostly with people who have never been here, but an image problem all the same. I can think of no place in the Alps where the reality is so much the polar opposite of common perception. 'The skiing is lousy,' they say. Nonsense. The linked areas of Mont Joly, Mont Joux, St Nicolas de Veroce, Le Bettex, Rochebrune, Côte 2000, Cret-du-Midi, Cristomet, and Praz sur Arly collectively represent more terrain than you can possibly ski in a week. 'The place is too low, it's not snow-safe.' Again, just not true. Because all the land is farm pasture it takes very little snow to constitute a good cover, and because of the

close proximity of Mont Blanc the snow normally lasts well into April. And even when there's no precipitation at all in the atmosphere, Megève benefits from a well-developed snow-making system. Nothing illustrates the bad snow myth as clearly as my own experience last January. Chamonix's Grands Montets was closed due to lack of snow while in nearby Megève the cover was of North American standard: plenty thick and perfectly groomed. 'Yes, but it's so Parisian,' they will say. Well if that means enjoying a morning coffee on the terrace of a café overlooking the picturesque historic town square, or that the shops are all of interesting and diverse appeal, that the antique stores are some of the best in the mountains, or that it has some of the finest restaurants in Europe, then perhaps yes it is Parisian − but I can't see that as anything other than a good thing. 'But surely all those fur coats are a bit over the top?' In the half dozen times I have been in Megève I can count the fur coats I have seen on one hand. Generally the dress code is appropriately casual.

It seems a little ridiculous to devote so much space to refuting Megève's fur coat image, but it's important to understanding the real Megève – a beautifully preserved Alpine village that's also a delightful place to ski. 'But surely all this beauty, charm and sophistication come at a price?' Well I confess I used to assume so too – until I discovered that one of the best places to stay in Megève is also the most affordable.

Au Coin du Feu was the original Sibuet hotel. Before Jean-Louis and Jocelyne Sibuet created their now famous Fermes de Marie, Lodge Park, Hotel Mont-Blanc, Cour des Loges in Lyon and La Bastide de Marie in Provence, they were the proprietors of this small timber-clad property in the middle of town on the road that leads to the main ski lift. In a sense, Au Coin du Feu was the laboratory for the successful Sibuet formula. The old timber, the cosy ambience, an abundance of Savoie craft, wood-panelled bedrooms, typical Savoyard fabrics – the Jocelyne Sibuet look was incubated in this three-star establishment. But besides aesthetics, it's also where they evolved their particular brand of mountain hospitality:

fresh cakes, pastries, hot chocolate and tea set out in the salon ready for the tired and hungry skier returning from a day on the slopes; a continuously roaring fire; a breakfast that goes far beyond the French tradition of coffee and croissant; and fine cuisine.

Today Au Coin du Feu has become the quiet achiever in their Compagnie des Hôtels de Montagne. It doesn't get anywhere near as much press as Les Fermes de Marie, and it doesn't attract the famous personalities to be spotted in Le Lodge Park. But most guests at Au Coin du Feu prefer it that way. By and large the crowd at this hotel do it the old-fashioned way: breakfast in ski gear, out the door by nine, and never back before four. Once on the slopes, Megève can offer something that you won't find anywhere else in the Alps – practically every goat shed, shack or timber hut you come across on the pistes has the wine list of a city establishment, and a menu to make many places in Paris seem positively shabby – and not a fur coat in sight.

---

address Au Coin du Feu, Route du Téléphérique de Rochebrune, 74120 Megève, France

t +33 (4) 5021 0494 **f** +33 (4) 5021 2015 **e** contact@coindufeu.com

room rates from € 160

l'alpage du pré rosset

Staying overnight in a mountain refuge is the purest Alpine experience you can have. The very word refuge – or in French, *alpage* – conjures images of Mother Nature at her frosty worst. Wild blizzards, waist-deep snow, biting winds – a refuge can be a life-saving haven from winter's fury. Despite the very functional nature of these remote huts, they ooze charm. Hollywood agrees: think of a film set in the mountains – *Cliffhanger*, *The Eiger Sanction*, *Treasure of the Sierra Madre* – whether the hero is Sly, Clint or even Bogey, eventually he ends up in a refuge.

Climbers' and skiers' refuges were first built by Alpine clubs to provide a place to pass the night for mountaineers stranded in remote locations. They are usually equipped with basic bedding and canned food that the refuge tenant pays for by leaving money in an Alpine version of a jam jar. It is assumed visitors will respect the traditional fellowship of the mountains – and even these days, they usually do.

But the real Alpine refuge is much older than this. For hundreds of years, long before the advent of mountain sports and ski vacations, the refuge played an important part in the life of high-altitude farmers. In summer they took their livestock to higher pastures, and then when the weather started to turn they would bring them back down again. However, the snows could come early, with little warning, and cows and farmer would find themselves knee-deep in September. Early snow may be great news for skiers, but for farmers it was potentially a disaster. Cows could not survive long in deep snow, not so much because of the temperature but because they couldn't graze. Thus farmers started to build high-altitude refuges, just in case. These were barns, big enough to accommodate animals and bales of hay as well as the farmer.

With the advent of warmer winters, better forecasting and less dependence on farming, this original refuge is in danger of disappearing. So it is ironic that one of the most authentic examples in the Haute Savoie has been rescued by ski tourism. When Jocelyne and Jean-Louis Sibuet first came across this high-altitude barn, their dream was to buy it for themselves and their children, to use predominantly in the summer. Friends came for long lunches on big timber tables and soon it was obvious that the retreat was so special it bewitched all who came. Like religion, the Sibuets felt compelled to share it, and so they began offering it as a special destination for their guests.

If you are staying at the Sibuets' Fermes de Marie, Coin du Feu, Lodge Park, Mont Blanc, or Fermes du Grand Champ then you are in on the best ski secret in the French Alps. The adventure starts in the picture-perfect village of Megève. After breakfast you put on your boots, throw your skis over your shoulders, and clunk your way along the snow-covered cobblestones of the elegant main square, past the onion-domed church to the ski lift that takes you from the centre of the town to the 2,000-metre (6,500-foot) peak of Rochebrune. To reach L'Alpage du Pré Rosset you have to get to the Rosset peak, and the only way to do that is to ski. It takes a couple of hours. For the adventurous the final descent is an exhilarating run off-piste; for the more cautious there's a small winding trail. Either way, the final destination is a slice of life as it was pre-skiing, pre-alpinism, pre-tourism – a lost valley where this refuge is the only structure to be seen.

L'Alpage is a faded grey hulk of old timber and huge stone fireplaces. There's no hot water on tap, no super cushy bathrooms, no toasty warm guest suites, no television, no minibars, no room service, no mod cons. What it does have is authenticity by the wooden bucket-load: a roaring fire in a fireplace that's of proportions more bovine than human, old wooden benches, old wooden floors, old wooden tables…in fact the only thing not made of old wood is the plates they serve lunch on. If you have been raised on bad but convenient mountain food – the shuffle-along-with-a-tray variety – this place will spoil you forever. Prepared by staff who skied their way here before you, the food is all about the specialities of the region: wild boar pâté on crusty bread, pasta with local wild mushrooms, venison, a wild salad, and local cheeses, all washed down with the excellent Haute Savoie red, Mondeuse. At the end of the day you can ski back to Megève or you can spend the night the way they used to: with a big fire, a thick bedcover, and a full bottle of Génépy, the local firewater.

address c/o Les Fermes de Marie, chemin de Riante Colline, 74120 Megève, France

t +33 (4) 5093 0310   **f** +33 (4) 5093 0984   **e** contact@fermesdemarie.com

room rates from € 175

le lodge park

In the mid-1700s Louis XV, king of France, commissioned a series of tapestries depicting idyllic Chinese scenes. He presented these to the Chinese Emperor, who was apparently delighted because the tapestries, to his eyes, were so very French. It's a tale that comes to mind when I think of Le Lodge Park in Megève. Decorated in a manner inspired by the deeply American Adirondack style, Le Lodge Park is uncannily French. In the hands of the very stylish Jocelyne Sibuet, all the twigs, antlers and mounted fish look so much like they belong here in France's Haute Savoie that it almost seems surprising that this style originated in the rugged mountains of upstate New York.

The reason Le Lodge Park works so well, I think, is because the style is appropriate. It is, as the French say, *sportif*. And sport is still most people's reason for escaping to the mountains. But just as important as the activities of the mountains is the style. What the Sibuets have understood very well is that the most powerful tools and the most important ingredients in creating an attractive hotel are image and ambience. The antler chairs upholstered in *faux* leopardskin, the cushions that feature little chipmunks, the cleverly arranged twigs, and rooms clad in old weathered logs might be dismissed by the architectural purist as decorative camouflage. But that would be missing the point.

These days to escape means to experience something out of the ordinary – something different, as different as possible from what we already have and know. Writer Alain de Botton is convinced that our romanticizing imaginations make it almost impossible for any travel destination to live up to expectations. I agree with him that this is definitely a pitfall of modern travel, but I don't agree that it's a foregone conclusion. The way to successfully satisfy imagination is with even more imagination. If a hotel is reduced to simply a place to sleep, a place to eat, and a place to return to, weary, at the end of the day, then yes, it is almost certain to disappoint. But the Sibuets' approach is different. They consciously set out to create an experience and everything thereafter: the decoration, the food, the service, the facilities, the art, the crockery, the china, and indeed the furniture are all ingredients that contribute to their overall recipe. They know that if a place is done well enough, it's not so important if it's authentic or even culturally relevant.

White birch, mounted deer, old books:
Le Lodge Park's main living area is a
fanciful version of a mountain library

The rugged yet cosy guestrooms are
panelled with split logs and many have
views of the town and pistes

Stairs from the lobby lead to the hotel's
own ski shop and spa centre (a place to
try the mountain-formulated treatments)

No hospitality ritual escapes Jocelyne Sibuet: breakfast at Le Lodge Park is livened up by her compote collection

Antlers, antlers, everywhere: the aesthetic of an American hunting lodge is dressed with a French sophistication

Big fish, big reputation – Le Lodge Park's restaurant has established itself in a town famous for its culinary standards

Le Lodge Park by origin is an early nineteenth-century six-storey building in the centre of town. It was never a barn or a farm, so you know that the log panelling in your third-floor bedroom isn't original. Nor do you imagine that the proprietors have managed to collect such a plethora of antlers by being prolific hunters. The concrete walls in the downstairs ski shop were never originally clad in the bark of a birch tree and the river that runs through Megève doesn't have on its beds any native stone resembling the riverstone used to build the fireplaces in the downstairs salon and the upstairs suites.

As some friends of mine recently observed in India, we are now so well off that we can afford to 'act out' the lifestyle we dream of for ourselves. And clearly, for many people who are both fond of skiing and fond of Megève, Le Lodge Park is exactly the right stage. In terms of the skiing, the hotel is perfectly placed. From the ski room it's just a brief stroll across the village square to the gondola that takes you to the base of Rochebrune. The hotel has its own in-house ski shop, repair shop and rental shop and there's a well-equipped spa that can make your post-ski recovery a relaxing experience free from the usual aches and pains that leave you feeling like an old cripple in the morning.

Not only is it perfect for skiing, but Le Lodge Park is also perfectly propped to allow you to live the life of a mountain man. Guestrooms are ruggedly clad in logs, the salon has more riverstone, hunting trophies and antler chairs than a lodge in Alaska – everything is arranged to make you feel like the last great mountaineer.

The moral is: never let the truth get in the way of a good story, and never let authenticity get in the way of creating a fantasy. For that's what Le Lodge Park is – a very comfortable fantasy. Because when it really comes down to it, the closest you'll get to roughing it here is a pang of deprivation when the restaurant runs out of foie gras.

address Le Lodge Park, 100, rue d'Arly, 74120 Megève, France
t +33 (4) 5093 0503   **f** +33 (4) 5093 0952   **e** contact@lodgepark.com
room rates from € 200

plumpjack

All day long they begged. It was a Saturday in Squaw Valley, California, site of the 1960 winter Olympics, and the torrent of callers wanting dinner reservations in PlumpJack's restaurant was non-stop. Often the tone turned desperate. 'But my secretary called from San Francisco – what do you mean I'm not on the waiting list? Put me on the waiting list. How long is the waiting list? Is there any point being on the waiting list?'

This energetic campaign to get a table by food-savvy San Franciscans gives some perspective on PlumpJack's success. San Francisco has a serious food and wine reputation, perhaps more so than any other US city, and the fact that PlumpJack is so sought-after is a huge compliment. This odd-sounding hotel began life as a very successful restaurant in San Francisco. When the property originally built to house the 1960 Olympic delegation in Squaw Valley became available, Bill Getty and Gavin Newsom seized the opportunity to create a hotel, complete with a sister restaurant to their PlumpJack Café in San Francisco. Until PlumpJack came along, Squaw Valley was little more than a day ski resort with a large carpark and a host of facilities left over from the Olympics. It was

a good place to ski but not a good place to stay. Even today, most ski guidebooks describe Squaw as a day mountain. They remain oblivious to the existence of PlumpJack, which is remarkable considering the rock star status of the restaurant, and also the fact that it is literally next to the cable car. Guests need only walk across a small wooden bridge to get to the lift. Easier still, your ski pass is available from the hotel's front desk. Squaw Valley is a bit of a West Coast secret. The skiing is expansive and challenging, the lift complex is the most technologically advanced in North America, and although, unlike Heavenly valley, it hasn't got a constant view of Lake Tahoe as you ski down, it doesn't have the crowds either.

And then there's the snow. Less than three hours drive from San Francisco, Squaw Valley is in the Lake Tahoe ski region, one of the best places for snow in North America. As they say in Tahoe, 'when it dumps, it dumps.' The same storm that might drop a foot and half of fresh powder in Utah will drop three times that in Tahoe. Often, the biggest issue for weekend skiers isn't the problem of not enough snow but too much, making for an arduous return home.

PlumpJack, the hotel, and Squaw Valley, the mountain, are an attractive combination.

Getting a table for dinner on Friday or Saturday is as unlikely as being allowed to smoke – unless you are a guest

On the same night, you can swim, skate and ski without leaving the mountain – how Californian is that?

PlumpJack could not possibly be any closer to the lifts, and the restaurant a legend in Squaw Valley

Squaw Valley was the site of the 1960 Winter Olympics. You can see Lake Tahoe from the Olympic summit

The interior of PlumpJack is rustic yet contemporary, combining concrete, velvet and wrought iron

When it dumps, it dumps. The Lake Tahoe region gets more snowfall than any other American ski resort

What's more, despite the scramble for a table at PlumpJack's restaurant, there are more venues here than one might think. There are two restaurants at the top of the mountain, reached by cable car. Many people bring their skis, their skates and their swimsuits, because also at the top, with a view over Lake Tahoe, there is an ice-skating rink and a swimming pool. First you skate, then you swim, then you have dinner, and after dinner you ski back down to PlumpJack via a floodlit trail.

The appeal of PlumpJack's design is that it makes no attempt to accommodate convention or nostalgia. You will not find logs on the walls, twig furniture, riverstone fireplaces, Navajo rugs or any other reference to the American West. The prevailing aesthetic is entirely its own – a kind of backyard-baroque Arts and Crafts with a rusty twist. The design firm of Leavitt-Weaver were given plenty of breathing space in the brief, and the whimsical, slightly theatrical look they came up with is very fresh – particularly in the snow. But this after all is

California, where the new and contemporary are not only appropriate, they are warranted. Rooms are spacious and appealingly sparse without being cold and uninviting. Similarly the bar and restaurant are modern but with a heavy element of texture. The approach continues on the adjoining terrace, where huge rough-cut slabs of granite are arranged haphazardly, as if they have just fallen off the mountain, dividing a space that might otherwise be too vast to be attractive.

PlumpJack is a real skiers' hotel. Not only is the lift across the street, but there is a comprehensive ski boutique at the far end of the lobby as well as one of the most advanced ski rental operatives in the American West. The only thing that didn't make sense to me was the name, a tribute to Shakespeare's Falstaff character. But when you consider the lengths people will go to get a table in the restaurant, the fact that it should be named after a character who really *loved* to eat suddenly seems wickedly appropriate.

address PlumpJack, 1920 Squaw Valley Road, PO Box 2407, Olympic Valley, CA 96146, USA

t +1 (800) 323 7666 **f** +1 (530) 583 1734 **e** svi@plumpjack.com

room rates from US $185

the home ranch

Round Mountain Ranch, Big Creek Ranch, Triple Diamond Ranch, Yampa Valley Ranch – Steamboat Springs is ranch country. These are not just big houses by another name, they are real working ranches. This part of Colorado is Marlboro Country in the snow. Everybody – and I mean everybody – wears cowboy boots, tooled leather belts with big shiny buckles and big hats. And everybody drives a pickup truck.

I grew up skiing on the East Coast, in New England, and I used to dream of going to Steamboat Springs. The horses in the snow, the white-capped red barns and the famous powder snow seemed like the ultimate combination. I couldn't wait to head out west with my skis, a Ford Bronco and a pair of Tony Llama boots. Alas my parents had other plans, and before I ever had a chance, we moved to Australia. So it was with great anticipation that I drove from Denver to Steamboat last winter.

Steamboat is situated on what they call high prairie, flat land that happens to be at an altitude of almost 9,000 feet (2,750 metres). Nowhere else in the world is there such a vast fertile plateau at such an altitude. (Bolivia has the Alto Plano, but it's a barren, sky-high desert.) The town of Steamboat Springs got its name in the mid-1800s, when trappers trudging up the Yampa River heard a gurgling sound that they thought was a steamboat, but which turned out to be natural hot springs. Until recently it was a cattle town. Its main street, lined with weathered clapboard houses, is broad enough to allow a herd to be driven through. Today, however, skiing and ski tourism are the chief business, and ski tourism demands facilities that Steamboat provides in a style that's more big city than rodeo. Most of the architecture owes more to Starbucks than the Last Chance Saloon. Brochures still feature cowboys and rustic red barns, but the reality is that the Wild West flavour doesn't extend much beyond the old town and main street.

What a pity! I was really looking forward to the whole cowboy cattle-ranch thing. But once out of Steamboat, on the road to tiny Clark, the fantasy was back on track. At the northern end of the Elk River valley, with Hahn's Peak in the distance, the Home Ranch is a step back in time. There are no condominiums or hotels or even houses in this area, just the odd ranch. The town of Clark is straight out of cowboy folklore. It has a general store, a saloon bar and a sign that says 'Welcome to Clark. Elevation 7,271 feet. Population ?' (It seems they never got around to counting.)

The only hangout is the local bar, where the menu is real cowpoke stuff: chicken fried steak, fried catfish sandwiches, and pork belly chilli.

In summer, you can ride one of the Home Ranch's 140 horses through the surrounding birch forest. In winter the emphasis changes to skiing. For downhill enthusiasts, it's a thirty-minute drive past all the other ranches back to Steamboat. Directly exposed to any weather travelling across America, particularly fronts from the Pacific – the ones that bring snow – Steamboat is the place where they invented the term 'Champagne powder'. The main mountain is smallish by European standards, but the real attraction for skiers is the back country – the off-piste terrain in the forest glades. Cross-country skiers need not leave the grounds of the Home Ranch. What serve as riding trails during the summer are groomed and transformed into miles of cross-country trails.

Most importantly, the Home Ranch is not a hotel that happens to resemble a ranch. It is a ranch and a home that graciously opens its doors to guests. Ken Jones (proprietor and, it is said, a bit of a horse whisperer) explains that the tradition of receiving guests on a ranch goes back to the very earliest settlers, who were always glad of the company and an extra pair of hands. The accommodation includes eight private cabins and six rooms in the main house. Eating here is truly a 'come and get it' cowboy experience. You rise in the morning to a roaring fire in the cosy dining room, and as you settle in to the panoramic view someone emerges from the kitchen and announces that they're making blueberry pancakes and would you like some. It's a 'what's on the griddle today' kind of breakfast. On Mondays the restaurant is often booked out because everyone 'around these parts' knows that Monday night is barbecue night. Ken himself gets behind the biggest barbecue kettle you've ever seen and all the cowboys flock in. How do I know they're cowboys? As they say on the high prairie, 'no matter what you wear, if you wear a cowboy hat on your head you'll be called a cowboy.'

address The Home Ranch, PO Box 822, 54880 RCR 129, Clark, Colorado 80428, USA

t +1 (970) 879 1780   **f** +1 (970) 879 1795   **e** info@homeranch.com

room rates from US $300

misani

St Moritz is probably the most famous ski resort of them all. It was the first Alpine destination made famous by British mountain enthusiasts, who began making the arduous journey here in the late 1800s. Since then its combination of stunning location, predominant sunshine (322 days per year according to the tourist office) and diversity of winter activity – polo in the snow, the famous Cresta Run, cross-country skiing on the lake – have made it one of Europe's most desirable (and expensive) winter resorts. Exclusive is the tag most often applied to St Moritz, and not just because of the prices but because it was and still is *the* place to be seen. Numerous stories of rich playboys, Hollywood sirens, and rocking royalty have debuted here. St Moritz is a non-stop upmarket soap playing against the spectacular setting of 4,000-metre (13,000-foot) Piz Bernina with a chain of frozen white lakes at its foot. It's *Dynasty* in the Alps. This is where Gianni Agnelli would hobble out of his helicopter to do some off-piste skiing, one leg famously gripped in a high-tech brace, the result of a dreadful Riviera car accident; where Stavros Niarchos, the Greek shipping magnate parked his business and his sons because he believed they should have some fun in every working day; where Gunter Sachs forged his reputation as über-playboy in the dungeon-like Kellers of the Dracula Club. The Shah of Iran, Farouk of Egypt, the Grimaldis of Monaco, the Savoys of Italy, and countless British dukes and lords have chosen this as their winter hangout. The British aristocracy in particular have made St Moritz events such as the Cresta Run – barrelling down a twisting ribbon of ice at obscene speeds – so much their own that until recently one could only pay in sterling for the privilege of risking your life in their company.

More than a century of legendary clientele has inevitably yielded legendary places to stay: the strangely gothic Badrutt's Palace Hotel, the Carlton, the Kulm, and Suvretta House. All are big five-star hotels with big reputations. But somehow they seem tired and old and a bit anachronistic against today's less disciplined ski culture. Skiing is no longer about the hop-hop metronome regularity of linked turns, and listening to Hans the instructor's constant reminders to 'bend the knees'. Borrowing from board-riding culture, skiing today is about doing what feels right and looks good.

For today's freer, more demanding skier, St Moritz still has a lot to offer – great skiing, particularly off-piste, and world-class people-watching. But an alternative to the 'old club' accommodation would be welcome. Enter the Misani. Situated in a plum-coloured building of quasi-Palladian appearance in the beautifully preserved village of Celerina, Misani is the breath of fresh air that St Moritz needed. Celerina is on the outskirts of town at the bottom of the Cresta Run. Admittedly it has no view of the lake, but that's compensated for by the proximity of the Marguns cable station and the fact that the village has only a handful of small hotels. Once upon a time Jürg Mettler, owner of the Misani, used to spend half his working life in a car commuting to and from work in Zurich. Then one day he had had enough, and he opted instead for the high-altitude lifestyle of St Moritz. Being an ex-urbanite he knew what this resort was missing, and he set out to plug the gap in the market.

Outside, the facade of Misani is handsome enough, but nothing remarkable. Inside, it's a different story. Avant-garde, edgy, irreverent and certainly different, Misani is a weird but wonderful mix of Alpine traditions with funky detail and modern touches. It has the wood-panelled *Stuben* and antler chandeliers we have come to expect as well as Italian-designed furniture, slick Euro-chic dining and utterly out-of-the-ballpark bedrooms. These are the design equivalent of world music, inspired by themes like the Marrakesh Medina, the American West, and the scorched earth of deserts. There are Arabic guestrooms that are all blue-green washed walls and mosaic inlaid tables; what the hotel calls 'Swiss modern' rooms in handwashed sunny yellow (more Swiss Family Robinson than Swiss Alps); and on the top floor, between the rafters, there are the wilderness rooms dedicated to the wild beauty of places as diverse as Montana and Rajasthan. With two restaurants and a bar, staying at the Misani doesn't feel like you are making too many sacrifices in lieu of those crusty old five stars. And with the money you are saving, you can be old-fashioned at least in one way – you can stay for a month.

address Misani, CH-7505 St Moritz-Celerina, Switzerland
t +41 (81) 833 3314 **f** +41 (81) 833 0937 **e** info@hotelmisani.ch
room rates from SFr 150

hotel saratz

'No fur coat?' Nobody goes to St Moritz without a fur coat, at least not according to my patrician uncle. Barely twenty years old, I was about to embark on my first Christmas and New Year in St Moritz. I thought he was kidding – this was a ski resort. Why would I need a fur coat? But my uncle insisted and in the end we settled for a fur-trimmed leather trenchcoat (very Frederick Forsyth) which he just happened to have hanging in his closet. My uncle was right, I should have guessed. Why be surprised about the fur coat when I had already packed a dinner jacket? Nobody goes to St Moritz without a tux – or a fur coat.

For someone raised on the pancakes and hamburgers culture of American skiing, and the crazy *Lederhosen* and Schnapps *Gemütlichkeit* of Austria, it was quite an eye-opener. Almost every evening it was jacket and tie for dinner, and on the other nights it was black tie. I couldn't decide whether the formality or the prices were more difficult to get used to. In the end the shock of the prices won. My first St Moritz ski vacation was an experience I will never forget. The main event of the fortnight was New Year's Eve at Badrutt's Palace Hotel. Champagne appeared only in magnums, and my dinner companion to the right, Lady 'Bubbles' Rothermere, who also happened to be the hostess, kept me amused by periodically dumping pieces of priceless jewelry in my lap which I was instructed to pin to the drapes behind us to make the place a little less drab. The party after the party was at Dracula's, favourite St Moritz haunt of those who can't sleep. There was not a table that was not being danced on and the magnums continued unabated. The crowd at St Moritz may be a nightmare for P.E.T.A. (People For the Ethical Treatment of Animals) but they sure know how to party.

St Moritz in season is something to experience at least once before you die. Apart from the glamour and the furs, the skiing is also pretty good. Even in a bad snow year, there is always the Corvatsch glacier, and with the right guide the off-piste is almost on a par with Chamonix. Then there is the food: it's almost impossible to have a bad meal in St Moritz, on or off the slopes. The precision for which the Swiss are famous is its key.

The only glitch is price. Paying crazy money can put a damper on almost anything, and it's the one significant drawback of skiing in St Moritz. The Saratz is the perfect solution:

185

a beautiful but affordable hotel situated in the heart of Pontresina, a charming little village just a stone's throw from St Moritz. You can go into town any time, and when you have seen one fur coat too many, the Saratz awaits as a comprehensively stylish retreat. The hotel is 125 years old and yet it's brand new. One of the first hotels in this old Engadine town, it was also one of the first to embrace modernity. It's an intelligent, attractive mix of the new and the old. The recently constructed stone block houses sixty-three guestrooms (all with plenty of closets and a view), the kindergarten, the health centre and the pool. The old part houses the dining room, the *Stube*, the jazz bar and reception. One indication of how well the two styles have merged is that most guests like to lounge in the modern section, while they prefer to eat in the more traditional spaces. The Saratz is one of a new generation of ski hotels that work even if there is no snow – or rather, especially if there is no snow. With a jazz bar, a library, two restaurants, three bars, a steam

room, swimming pool, games arcade, and a modern lobby with a fireplace, you will never be bored – even if global warming does reduce the winter cover.

Formal and informal, funky and traditional, quiet and lively – the Saratz was conceived in full recognition that the new generation hotel guest wants it all, and the new generation skier is no exception. You can breakfast in the rather grand Victorian ballroom, then burn some calories in the enormous indoor pool housed in a double-storey glass atrium that offers a magnificent view of the surrounding mountains. Got a couple of rambunctious rug rats? Not a problem: drop them off at the professionally staffed kindergarten. On a blue-sky day you can lunch on the terrace of the hotel's cosy café, and after hours the Saratz bar is *the* place to hang out in Pontresina. So it should come as no surprise that there are reports of a new breed of winter guest checking into Hotel Saratz: ones who don't ski at all.

address Hotel Saratz, CH-7504 Pontresina/St Moritz, Switzerland

t +41 (81) 839 4000 **f** +41 (81) 839 4040 **e** info@saratz.ch

room rates from SFr 280

sundance

The sign on Interstate 15 to Salt Lake City pointed to Sundance. I took the turn-off and immediately started to worry. If Sundance was signposted so prominently perhaps it wasn't the perfectly preserved little mountain hideaway I had hoped for. Less than forty minutes later, my fears were put to rest. My rentacar was slipping backwards down a narrow mountain pass at an alarming rate, and another car coming down had just slid into the canyon's creek. Even big rugged four-wheel drives were coming down the twisting mountain road like toboggans. Believe it or not, this mayhem was a welcome sign. Here was a mountain road that looked like a mountain road, unlike the six-lane freeways to resorts like Vail, Colorado. If the road isn't compromised, I thought, then the place itself probably isn't either.

I was right. Located on the slopes of the breathtaking 12,000-foot (3,600-metre) Mount Timpanogos, Sundance is as authentic as the treacherous road that leads there. Robert Redford's commitment to the environment and his sensitivity to the creative process – to design, architecture and landscaping – make it unique in the American West. It all started over thirty years ago, when Redford was looking for a place to live and raise his children. It was

known as Timphaven then, a small ski resort tucked away in the folds of Utah's spectacular Wasatch Mountains. Redford knew the terrain and he decided to purchase a parcel of land to build a house for his wife and family. But the close proximity to Salt Lake City worried him. He feared it was only a matter of time before property developers stepped in and ruined the place. So he made a trip to New York and managed to secure enough investors to buy the entire valley. That way he could ensure that Sundance, as he renamed it, would stay just as it was.

The name refers to a ritual of the local Ute Indians – but obviously also pays tribute to one of Redford's most memorable roles in *Butch Cassidy and the Sundance Kid*. Appropriately enough, Sundance is a place that was created with a film director's eye. Wherever you look, from the strategically placed Native American art and Wild West craft, to the rustic barn-like architecture, the carefully landscaped paths that connect cabins and restaurants, even the graphics on the staff t-shirts, it's clear that compromise is not a word Redford chooses to be familiar with. The Owl Bar, for instance, is the original 1890s rosewood bar rescued from Thermopolis, an old Wyoming town once

THE OWL BAR

Sundance, Utah

OPENING TIMES

MONDAY - FRIDAY 4:00 PM ~ 12:00 AM

frequented by Butch Cassidy's Hole in the Wall gang. There are also two restaurants, the Tree Room and the Foundry Grill, as well as the General Store, the skier's Snack Shack, and the equipment rental shop. Sundance has been an evolving project since 1969. The first job was to get rid of the remnants of Timphaven, which included a 1960s burger joint named Ki-Te-Kai, Samoan for 'come and get it'. The only thing that has survived from old Timphaven is Ray's Lift, which is still called Ray's Lift.

As far as the skiing goes, I was without expectations. But it snowed all night and the potential for fresh tracks was motivation to set the alarm early. Much as many locals will not thank me for exposing their secret – Sundance is simply a great place for experiencing Utah's legendary powder. It's true there's only one lift, but it goes for miles and ultimately takes you to a mountain that's surprisingly steep and with surprisingly long runs. My absolute favourite is Bishop's Bowl, which ends in a long half-pipe-like gully. In larger resorts such a beautiful

open bowl would be 'skied out' in minutes. At Sundance they limit the number of people on the mountain, meaning the powder possibilities are preserved for longer.

The plan from the beginning was to make Sundance both a recreational and an arts community. It was not all, as one might assume, smooth sailing. In Redford's own words: 'The first year I couldn't get a loan from the bank. The waiters didn't show up…. Vehicles stalled, sewers backed up, we were robbed, and the tree in the Tree Room died.' Despite all, Redford has managed not only to maintain the beauty of the place but to preserve the character of a small local village. A guy I met in the Owl Bar had been skiing here since before it was Sundance and more than thirty years later it's still his favourite mountain. 'You should see it on a Sunday,' he said with a grin, 'it's the best place to ski in the entire Rockies.' Why Sunday? Because Provo, the nearest town, ten minutes down the road, is ninety per cent Mormon – and Mormons do not ski on Sundays.

address Sundance, RR3, A-1 Sundance, Utah 84604, USA

t +1 (801) 225 4100 **f** +1 (801) 226 1937 **e** Reservations@Sundance-Utah.com

room rates from US $245

wyndham peaks

I remember Telluride from my childhood. My father was doing field work in the Colorado Rockies and we were camped with caravan and tent in the small mountain town of Ouray, a former mining camp in the San Juans now better known for its hot springs. We had a jeep and on weekends we would go adventuring along what they called jeep trails. Apart from the thrill of not knowing if you would come home alive, the fun was in discovering high altitude ghost towns. Some were ramshackle, barely more than a collection of derelict huts, but the most impressive was Telluride. It still had its saloon bar, a general store, an opera house, a town hall and a few banks, all from its Victorian heyday. The whole place looked like a set from *The Good, the Bad and the Ugly*. It wasn't completely a ghost town, it's true. Some people were living there and you could still get a drink in the old saloon. Telluride, however, had certainly seen better days. Once its nearby silver and gold deposits had made many a prospector rich, but by then the only asset it had left was its spectacular location. Situated in a remote southwestern corner of the Colorado Rockies, this is one of very few American towns that can compete with the European Alps for sheer visual drama. Telluride is nestled in a deep

valley, and surrounded by the 14,000-foot (4,300-metre) peaks of the San Juan range: craggy, pointed, foreboding and enormously impressive.

It was only a matter of time before this majestically situated town was rediscovered. Indeed, since the mid-eighties, Telluride has not just been rediscovered, it has experienced what can only be described as a second gold rush. Within less than twenty years it has become one of North America's most celebrated ski destinations. Had you happened to own a simple clapboard Victorian house in the old town, then you would now be a millionaire. Telluride is once again a boomtown. It boasts more excellent restaurants than the average big city, many of the world-class quality that one normally associates with places like Manhattan. But then with a transient population that at any one time includes more than its fair share of America's movers and shakers, that shouldn't come as a surprise. To accommodate the jet set, Telluride even hosts its own airport – the highest in the northern hemisphere.

Until very recently, the only aspect of Telluride that didn't bask in universal acclaim was the skiing. It had limited potential, and by Colorado standards, not particularly impressive

vertical. All that changed in 2002 with a seventy-five per cent expansion of skiable terrain. New high-speed quad chairs give access to what is known as Prospect Bowl, where the skiable elevation goes to 12,250 feet (3,700 metres), leading down to Telluride station at 8,750 feet (2,600 metres). In total 733 new acres have been added, serviced by three high-speed quads. And as in Europe, the slopes lead all the way back to the streets of the old town itself.

There is also a new side to the town of Telluride, called the Mountain Village. Situated at 10,000 feet (3,000 metres), this is where you will find the Wyndham Peaks Resort. In contrast with the quaint, unpretentious timber architecture of the old town, the Peaks, at first glance, is a bit of a shock. It's a huge, unapologetic hulk of a building, like a giant apartment block in the snow. But considering that there was nothing here before, it's not so out of place – at least it's not trying to disguise itself as a multi-storey log cabin. It is what it is – a large complex whose size is a gauge of just how much it has to offer. It is the complete ski hotel, perhaps more so than any other in North America. It has its own ski shop, its own rental shop, a special counter for lift passes, two restaurants, an outdoor pool, an indoor pool, a lap pool, a weight gym, a free weights gym, an aerobic gym, convention spaces, a Golden Door Spa centre offering a catalogue of treatments, and a four-storey-high lobby called the Great Space which is one of *the* places to hang out in Telluride. Despite its size, the Peaks has real atmosphere. There is live music in the early evening – blue grass and country, of course – and a fireplace big enough for a buffalo.

Given its hulking size, I admit I was prepared to dislike Wyndham Peaks. But the longer I stayed, the more I was seduced by the luxury of so many facilities. The sheer convenience of stepping out of the lift one floor below the Legends breakfast restaurant and straight into your skis and onto the slopes is enough to convince the most sceptical ski connoisseur.

---

address Wyndham Peaks Resort, 136 Country Club Drive, Telluride, Colorado 81435, USA

t +1 (970) 728 6800 **f** +1 (970) 728 3291 **e** dbessera@wyndham.com

room rates from US $189

dunton hot springs

The story of how Christoph Henkel and Bernt Kuhlmann, former LA-based film producers, turned an abandoned mining camp into one of the most exclusive mountain retreats in the US has become the stuff of hotel legend. Bang in the middle of one of the most pristine and spectacular stretches of Rocky Mountain wilderness and flanked by no less than three 'fourteeners' – local jargon for 14,000-foot (4,000 metre) peaks – Dunton is blessed not just by breathtaking scenery and a plethora of natural hot springs, but also by the exquisitely eccentric taste of its cosmopolitan proprietors. Bits and pieces from the family *Schloss* outside Salzburg, African ceremonial cloth, beautifully weathered Santa Fe furniture, Navajo bedspreads and a truckload of Turkish kilims decorate a dozen cabins that still look dishevelled and forgotten on the outside, but never had it so good inside.

Yet everybody laughed in 1993 when the two friends decided to buy the entire town. Once there had been silver in this remote stretch of the San Juans, but now there was only the fortune-hunters' detritus: a bunch of crudely constructed log cabins, a dancehall with a caved-in roof, and a saloon bar. But as far as Kuhlmann and Henkel were concerned,

'there was treasure in them there hills'. They didn't see a run-down ghost town, they saw the makings of a romantic fantasy. And that's exactly what Dunton became. In fact so effective were the two bachelors at recreating the romance of the wild Wild West that it worked on them before the first guests ever checked in. Within months of acquiring the old camp they had each proposed and shortly afterwards married. Bernt and his Colorado-born wife Cat even got hitched right here in the outdoor chapel next to the town's own 115-foot (35-metre) waterfall. By the time Dunton's fairy-tale transformation was complete, both Bernt and Cat and Christoph and Katrin (a Munich-based dealer in fine art) had between them produced a brood of little Duntonians.

Spurred on perhaps by a new level of domesticity, they left no stone unturned in making the individual cabins of Dunton *le dernier cri* in indulgent luxury. The natural slate floors are heated from below and the telecommunications are of a big-city sophistication. There are three hot-spring bathing venues (one outside, one inside and one in a teepee) and a two-level library built by Christoph for Katrin as a wedding present.

A truckload of Turkish kilims were used to decorate the renovated cabins that host guests at Dunton Hot Springs

Dunton is a former mining camp in the spectacular wilderness of the southern San Juan ranges of the Colorado Rockies

Dunton is blessed with an abundance natural hot springs. Guests can swim a 40°C pool inside an old log cabin

n the outside, the rough, rugged and eathered prospectors' cabins appear untouched

Inside, the shacks are a haven of comfort and style, decorated with Santa Fe antiques and old trapper's snow shoes

Dunton, flanked by no less than three 14,000-foot (4,300-metre) peaks, lies in an untouched mountain playground

Guests enjoy the privacy of their own cabin, but at mealtimes people meet in the saloon bar and the dancehall is the venue for the odd barn dance or concert. Last year it hosted a Jamaican steel-drum band.

The resurrection of Dunton is a great story. But what seems to escape almost all the magazines and newspapers that have dedicated significant column inches to it is that Dunton is one of the best heli-skiing destinations in North America. Skiing in impossibly remote areas with the aid of helicopters is usually associated with the Canadian Cariboos, where there are lodges specializing in nothing but. It's the ultimate in skiing – no argument. The only problem is that – to quote an old line – 'there's no *there* there'. You stay in the middle of nowhere, you are dropped by chopper into the middle of nowhere, you ski to the middle of nowhere, and at the end of the day you return to your isolated purpose-built box in the middle of nowhere. Not only is it slightly disorientating, it also seems a tiny bit

pointless. Canadian heli-skiing offers plenty on the adrenalin-pumping adventure side, but is very light on the more seductive pleasures of life. Dunton heli-skiing is totally different. The choppers land in the centre of town and take you to any one of the surrounding peaks. After a few runs you stop at a vantage point where on a clear day you can see the deserts and canyons flanking these mountains, which remain snow-capped even in August. The last run of the day takes you right back to the old town, where the bubbling hot springs are the perfect antidote to the day's exertions.

It's not just the luxury or the rustic romance that define the Dunton experience. More than anything it's the extremely rare opportunity to enjoy Mother Nature's high-altitude perfection without having to share it with too many others. Here you really can pretend, if only for a short while, that these magnificent mountains are yours. But remember: if you are a bachelor and you want to stay that way, come alone.

---

address Dunton Hot Springs, PO Box 818, Dolores, Colorado 81323, USA

t +1 (970) 882 4800 **f** +1 (970) 882 7475 **e** info@duntonhotsprings.com

room rates from US $400

village montana

Officially, the ski area is called Espace Killy. Once upon a time these slopes were known as Tignes and Val d'Isère, but ever since Jean-Claude Killy – 1968 Grenoble Winter Olympics triple gold medallist – exhausted himself organizing the 1992 Albertville Olympics, the authorities decided to rename this legendary ski destination in his honour.

Trouble is, I have yet to come across a skier who announces that he or she is off to Espace Killy for a skiing vacation. Most people still know it as Tignes-Val d'Isère. But whatever the name, my impression of Tignes has always been rather mixed. The skiing is great – some of the best, the longest and most challenging in the world, especially off-piste – but the flipside is Tignes itself. Tignes-le-Lac looks like an East German Cold War housing project, and Haute Tignes (slightly higher up) is even worse. It sounds severe, even unkind, but I challenge anyone who has been there to disagree: great skiing, shame about the aesthetics.

Before the advent of ski tourism, this was a poor but spectacular part of the Savoie. Tignes-le-Lac and Haute Tignes didn't exist at all. Like all traditional Alpine settlements, the original town of Tignes is located much further down, below the tree line. Higher than 1,200

or 1,300 metres (4,000–4,300 feet) it was too cold to live or keep animals, with too much snow and no trees for protection. However, the growth of mass ski tourism has completely changed attitudes to altitude. The search for bigger, higher and longer ski runs, preferably with guaranteed snow, has long since lured developers into the expansive treeless terrain above old settlements. Appropriate architecture was much lower on their priority list than ability to pack them in. Back in the 1960s, the world was looking forward, and concrete was the material of the future. Concrete can sometimes, in the hands of a very gifted architect, be plastic poetry. But unlike timber, it gets worse not better as it gets older. Four decades on in places like Tignes we must live with the unsightly consequences.

Today we are so spoilt we demand all the mod cons – the indoor as well as the outdoor swimming pool, at least two restaurants (heaven forbid that we don't have a choice), cable TV (preferably digital), and state-of-the-art telephone, fax and email facilities. What's more, we also want the romance and cosiness that Alpine traditions bring: the weathered timbers, red-and-white gingham, wing chairs by the fire, cowbells and old clocks above it.

Village Montana is brilliantly located: ski in, ski out, and out of sight of the architectural eyesore of Tignes-le-Lac

Wherever possible, the interiors feature traditional Savoyard details such as this built-in alcove bed

Elsewhere, old wood and tradition are the decorative keys; in the bathrooms the style is Gaudí à la Provence

very room is a suite and every suite has a living area with fireplace. Leaving your room is the first day's challenge

Lots of snow covering lots of wood: Village Montana looks exactly like one expects an Alpine hotel to look

Old doors, old wood, new idea: aged timber works wonderfully well in Montana's Alpine interiors

But are we prepared to give up the big snow-safe pistes for all that? No way. It has to be ski in, ski out, and preferably bang on the slopes. It's a tall order: skiers want tradition and heritage in locations that never had them in the first place.

Yet on almost all counts, Village Montana succeeds. Firstly it's situated well away from the high-rise mess of Tignes-le-Lac, on a slope that takes in the most dramatic view of the entire terrain. The steepest and highest slopes are spotlit after dark, so even at night there's a spectacle from your balcony. Inside, the eye rests on plenty of weathered wood. You know that a large building like this, with elevators and underground carpark, can't really be old, but it's convincingly cosy. The public areas follow the typically rustic style of the Savoie – agreeable, even if nothing noteworthy in terms of innovation. Where this hotel truly distinguishes itself, however, is in the rooms. All are suites – more like apartments than the usual little box you get in the mountains.

No more climbing over gear to get to your bed: here you actually have room for all the paraphernalia you have to lug along. Some suites are duplex with two bedrooms, a separate living area upstairs, two bathrooms, and what must be the ultimate – a private sauna in the bathroom. One-bedroom apartments are equally spacious, and without exception all have a fireplace. Weathered furniture and warm fabrics complete a set-up so cosy that you might be tempted not to leave your room after hours. That would be a shame, because Montana is quite a complex. It has an outdoor pool, an indoor pool, a huge hammam, three restaurants and two bars.

Stylewise, Village Montana goes a long way towards reclaiming the heritage of the region. It will never win awards for design innovation – although the Andalusian-inspired pool is rather attractive. But that's not the point. For the first time there's a venue in Tignes that matches up to the skiing – without looking like an Ostbloc sanatorium.

---

address Village Montana, Les Almes, 73320 Tignes-le-Lac, Savoie, France

t +33 (4) 7940 0144 **f** +33 (4) 7940 0403 **e** contact@vmontana.com

room rates from € 272

ansitz heufler

The Pustertal in Südtirol looks exactly like you would expect the perfect piece of Austria to look – except that it's in Italy. It is a seemingly endless series of idyllic valleys surrounded by towering snow-capped peaks and countless postcard villages with nothing taller in view than the church steeple. After a while you learn to distinguish one Hansel-and-Gretel *Dorf* from the next by the shape of its church – which was the reason they were all built slightly different in the first place. Each time I've been to the Pustertal, or in Italian La Pusteria, I've been captivated by its unspoilt charm. And yet every perfect little farmhouse I passed, every slightly decrepit timber barn or traditionally painted house, I was frustrated by the fact that I hadn't found the architectural equal of the area's natural beauty. It turned out I wasn't looking hard enough.

Here and there, usually on the crest of a hill or some other strategic point, you will find a *castello* or *Schloss*, the reinforced castles of the Alps. All were built in the days when this mountain world was divided into hundreds if not thousands of fiefdoms. Because of the long mountain winters, the Alpine Schloss had very small windows, very thick walls, and interiors that were a kind of 'Bauer Baroque' (*Bauer* is the German word for farmer). For despite their aristocratic function, on the inside these castles maintained a close relationship to the traditional farmhouse.

Ansitz Heufler is such a Schloss, and has a long and impressive history. Through wars and intermarriage and political intrigue, the Ansitz has changed hands so often within a complex web of interrelated family trees that it would take a page just to list all its past proprietors. Suffice to say that this castle has a colourful past. Building began in 1580 on the distinctive three-storey structure with square corner towers, and it remains largely unchanged today. Chiselled into the masonry surrounding the massive wooden entrance is the date 1598, which corresponds to the year that Kaiser Rudolph II gave the Heufler family the right to use their title for the new property. Despite changes in the area's overlords – for a time Bavaria, then Austria again, then Italy – and despite numerous smaller power struggles, the Ansitz has suffered little more than a few minor battle scars in its massively thick walls and some internal damage when troops were stationed here during World War I.

The Steiner family that run the old Schloss today are not related to the Heuflers. They are

hotel professionals. For guests, that is good news – there's no trace of family hobby about Ansitz Heufler. It is run by Thomas Steiner, a hotel-school graduate with experience in some of Europe's best Alpine hotels, while his brother Michl is in-house chef. In a remarkably short space of time the two young enthusiasts have emphatically put the place on the culinary map. The food is inventive, original and contemporary. There are traditional dishes on the menu – like the local pasta speciality, a ravioli filled with quark and spinach – but the reason the restaurant attracts people from all over La Pusteria is its readiness to take culinary risks. The youthful energy of the Steiner brothers is balanced by Frau Steiner's natural sense of mountain hospitality. The matriarch of the Steiner family, she gives the guestrooms a welcome feminine touch in the perfectly made beds, carefully arranged down pillows, the crisply ironed hand-embroidered table linens and the colour-coordinated details of the decor. It's also Frau Steiner who makes sure that

dining tables are never without candelabra and that there are freshly baked cakes, hot chocolate and tea waiting in one of the historic *Stuben* when guests get back from the slopes.

During the day you ski the Kronplatz, only ten minutes from Ansitz Heufler, where a comprehensive network of state-of-the-art snow-making machines ensures you never need worry about the pistes. For skiers craving variety, Cortina is forty-five minutes away and the extensive area of Val Gardena less than an hour. At night you return to a real Schloss to warm your toes by the huge fire in the bar, a cosy vaulted space that used to be the castle's smoking room where meats were cured for winter. The pitch black colour of the walls is not paint but the effect of centuries of smoke and soot seeping into their porous stone. And that's what is so captivating about this place – it's real. The walls are uneven, the old iron locks stick, floors creak, and the vast, dim hallways echo with the ghosts of more than five centuries of Austro-Italian mountain men.

---

address Ansitz Heufler, Oberrasen 37, I–39030 Rasen im Antholzertal, Italy

t +39 (0474) 498 582   **f** +39 (0474) 498 046   **e** info@heufler.com

room rates from € 52

gannerhof

The Villgratental in Austria's Osttirol is the one that got away. Somehow this mountain valley has totally escaped the all-embracing grip of Austrian ski tourism. Innervillgraten, the village located in the Villgraten valley, consists almost entirely of three- and four-hundred-year-old farmhouses. The only exceptions are the church and the town hall. Farming and timber, not tourism, are the industries of this valley.

Until 1962, the grandfather of the present proprietor of Gannerhof was a farmer. For his son, however, three cows and a paddock were not enough; he sidestepped family tradition, and that's how his son, Herr Mühlmann, came to run Gannerhof. He too was a farmer at first until he decided he could do better by turning his inheritance from farmhouse to guesthouse. Local bankers didn't think it was a good idea at all: who would come? And what for? All the valley could offer was farmhouses and the odd timber yard…. They were right of course, but as locals they didn't appreciate that unspoilt Alpine valleys are not as common as they used to be. Bankers be damned, Mühlmann pursued his dream. The old family *Bauernhaus* yielded eleven basic but handsome guestrooms, a new *Stube*, two old *Stuben* (one originally from the 1700s), a new kitchen and a sauna where the

chickens used to live. The Gasthof Gannerhof opened for business in 1992. It didn't take long for a local wit to point out that there was one *hof* too many in Innervillgraten – a dig at the rather awkward name. Point taken, the Mühlmanns dropped the Gasthof part and decided to use the single appellation without a der, die or das to spoil its simplicity.

It was clear that the Mühlmanns were going to do things their own way. Although Alois and Monika always intended to base Gannerhof's cuisine on local fresh farm produce, they had not actually planned on doing the cooking. But one night, the chef didn't show and Frau Mühlmann stepped in. That was more than eighteen years ago. Not only is she still in the kitchen, but she has made quite a name with her unique and *ländlich* cuisine. At Gannerhof they bake their own bread, churn their own butter, and even grow the herbs to make their own *Kräutertee* (herbal tea). Ducks, chickens, geese, goats: everything on the menu, if not straight from the backyard, is reared in the valley. The animals are part of the ambience, and some guests have grown very attached to them. One couple were particularly anguished to discover – half-way through dinner – that they were eating their friend Ushi the duck.

Although Alois only lasted two years in farming, its culture is clearly in his blood. There is definitely a farmer's mentality in his and his wife's straightforwardness and decency. For example, much as I wanted to photograph other bedrooms, they would not allow it out of respect for their guests' privacy even though they were all off skiing. Frau Mühlmann was a bit surprised by my enthusiasm. 'They are just bedrooms,' she said, 'they have a bed and a place to hang your clothes, nothing more!' Given that some of the rooms feature Grandpa Alois's antiques, and others, such as the top-floor apartment, combine a simple pine interior with the avant-garde artistry of a local blacksmith, such modesty was a surprise.

Despite all the awards and commendations the kitchen at Gannerhof has garnered over the years, no one outside of Austria seems to have ever heard of it. It's extraordinary. Perhaps the Austrians from nearby Lienz are keen to keep Gannerhof to themselves. Interestingly, despite its isolation, and despite the fact that

Innervillgraten has no ski shops, no boutiques, no ski service or rental, the local skiing area – less than ten minutes away – is one of the biggest in Osttirol. The south-facing pistes of the Hochpustertal are only a ten-minute drive from Gannerhof. And for advanced skiers looking for a challenge, the 3,000-metre (9,000-foot) peaks of the Hohe Tauern are less than a half an hour away. Gannerhof represents an extremely rare opportunity to combine the ambience and cuisine of an authentic Austrian *Bauernhaus* with some excellent skiing in the Eastern Alps.

Frau Mühlmann has a great story: one day, a lady from Germany called and wanted to know what there was to do for the children. 'Nothing,' replied Monika. 'What do you mean, nothing?' asked the caller. 'Nothing. Our children were raised in and around this house, there are fields to run in and animals and mountains, but beyond that nothing.' 'Good,' the caller replied, 'that is exactly what I am looking for.'

---

address Gannerhof, A-9932 Innervillgraten 93, Austria

t +43 (4843) 5240 **f** +43 (4843) 5506 **e** gannerhof@aon.at

room rates from € 58

madlein

Every year Ischgl, a Tirolean village in the long and narrow Paznaun Valley, not too far from the Vorarlberg, attracts big-name entertainers for end-of-season open-air concerts. Last year it was Sting; in previous years Bob Dylan, Rod Stewart, Tina Turner, Mick Jagger and Elton John have all performed here. During the season, Ischgl's upmarket hotels cater predominantly to Germans and Scandinavians, and the town's après-ski is legendary. A Coyote Ugly Bar is hardly what you would expect of a traditional Austrian village, but there they are, nightly, young girls performing athletically – for want of a better word – on the bars.

This place is also no slouch when it comes to the skiing. Combining the Swiss resort of Samnaun and Austrian Galtur, this *Riesengebiet* has one of the fastest, most extensive and efficient lift systems in Europe. There's a seemingly endless choice of intermediate-level pistes, and the grooming is on a par with that of top North American resorts. The slopes are like carpet, and the area also does extremely well in terms of annual snowfall. From the village of Ischgl at 1,400 metres (4,600 feet), a series of high-speed gondolas whisk you to the summit of Idalp, from where no less than fourteen high-speed chair lifts disperse skiers to a collection of peaks ranging from 2,300 to 2,800 metres (7,500–9,200 feet). Even a really well-travelled skier couldn't fail to be impressed by this area. And yet few people have heard of it. All the ski guidebooks agree that it is one of the most underrated resorts in Austria.

I was one of those skiers who did not know Ischgl. Perhaps it's the way the word is spelled, with all its consonants – it almost looks like a typing error. But then with a name like Ypma, I should talk. What drew me to Ischgl was actually not the skiing, but the Hotel Madlein. They sent me a fold-out poster of a dramatic-looking woman against a black background, and a series of interior impressions that looked like they came from Tokyo, not the tradition-rich and conservative Austrian Alps. Naturally I was intrigued. What was a Zen-inspired hotel doing in the Paznaun Valley?

The what and the why were quickly answered on meeting Günther Aloys, Madlein's proprietor. With his long grey hair and monochrome Prada wardrobe, he certainly didn't meet the stereotype of the traditional Austrian hotelier. Günther Aloys is the creative maestro who pioneered Ischgl's rock concerts. Locally, he is known as the art director of the Austrian Alps, and his daring ideas have earned

him recognition far beyond his valley. With Madlein, he wanted to start 'preparing for the guest of tomorrow'. His successes with concerts and the Ibiza-style Ischgl Pascha Disco had tuned him in to how acutely aware today's travellers are of fashion and style trends. That people are drawn by innovation and individuality in hotels is now well-established, particularly in the urban context – but in an Austrian mountain resort? Who was to know? The Aloys family experiment was not without risk. Yet to Günther Aloys's credit, he made no compromise. The Zen theme was chosen because it signifies both strength and beauty: qualities equally compatible with the Alps. Guestrooms are spare, light, spacious and wholly unconventional, with a glass-enclosed bathroom in the middle of the loft-like space. The materials reflect the mountains: stone, glass, and wood are the primary ingredients. Aloys would be the first to admit that his experiment is minimalistic, but the Madlein mantra is that discipline leads to freedom.

The Zen signature really comes into its own in the hotel's spa complex. Through a massive wall of floor-to-ceiling glass, the pool, the recovery area, the gym, the juice bar, the sauna and the steam room all look out on a Japanese garden usually covered in a light dusting of snow and always framed by the imposing peaks of the Tirol. Enormous slabs of light-grey granite, simple off-white canvas cushions and furniture in grey-faded teak complete a decor that is at once soothing and inspiring. It feels completely at home in these mountains, and most guests seem to think so too. Since the opening of Madlein's design rooms, they have been so in demand that there are plans to expand the concept to all the remaining, more traditional rooms of the hotel.

The Aloys family experiment is a triumph. And the reassuring irony of the Madlein success story is that no matter how innovative the design or progressive the theory, it all still remains part of an enduring Austrian tradition – the family hotel.

address Hotel Madlein, A-6561 Ischgl, Tirol, Austria

t +43 (5444) 5226 **f** +43 (5444) 5226 202 **e** info@ischglmadlein.com

room rates from € 98

the summit lodge

The blonde was holding a sign. Better still, it had my name on it. My flight from Reno had just landed in Vancouver. After a day of airports and security searches, things were looking up. I was on my way to Whistler, one of the legendary destinations for serious skiers. The blonde was my driver, sent by the Summit to take me to Whistler in a huge black four-wheel drive SUV (Sports Utility Vehicle) with tinted windows. I didn't know much about this new hotel, but already I was feeling optimistic.

The car turned out to belong to a transport company called Extreme Limousine. Since the drive to Whistler is one of the most spectacular in the world, the idea is that the ski adventure should start at the airport. Leaving Vancouver the road follows an amazing stretch of the Pacific coastline all the way to Whistler, winding its way around fjords framed by snow-capped forests. Alas, by the time we were on the road, it was dark, so there was no point in making off-road excursions along the way. But my driver turned out to be a keen skier, so for the duration of the drive we discussed the phenomenal changes the ski resort of Whistler has experienced in the past decade. I hadn't been here in over ten years and she told me I wouldn't recognize the place. On the

mountain they have added even more high-speed quad lifts, taking the total to far more than any other ski destination in North America. The village too has more than doubled in size. The Whistler I remember was quaint, small and quiet; the new Whistler is a mini-city with more restaurants, shops and cafés than a Californian shopping mall. By the time we pulled up to the hotel I was feeling depressed. What if the drive and the reputation had created expectations that wouldn't be fulfilled? But it had been a long day and it might all be different in the morning.

Things started to look up the minute I got to my room, which was more like an apartment. Fireplace, living room, kitchen – it had facilities and space that are not exactly commonplace in ski hotels. The next morning was even better: it was snowing and everything was fairy-tale white. The pine trees framed by my living-room window were sugar-coated, and with restored enthusiasm I headed down to breakfast. But after a fruitless search for the restaurant I discovered there wasn't one – not yet, anyway. The receptionist advised me that there were plenty of Starbucks nearby…. It turned out the Summit was so new they still had to find a sub-contractor to take on the in-house restaurant.

To be fair, the hotel was not quite finished when I was there: they were still experimenting with the lobby, the restaurant was still a vacant space, and the ambience was more apartment-block than buzzy hotel. However, its basic bones were already the best in Whistler. The rooms are gigantic, and the developers, an Asian property group, were keen to leave nothing out in terms of mod cons: wide-screen cable TV, computer terminals, state-of-the-art bathrooms, comprehensively equipped kitchens. What's more, with a 'meditation library', yoga classes, spa treatments and ambient aromatherapy, your après-ski wellbeing is amply provided for. The Summit Lodge has a management company that I'm confident by the start of the 2002–3 season will have filled in the gaps in their trademark hip and cosy manner. The Kimpton Group operates a whole string of properties in the United States. It has a reputation for a lifestyle signature that combines landmark restaurants with chic contemporary hotel rooms. At the Summit it was evident I was a tad too early, but the potential is certainly there.

In any case, the Summit Lodge can't go far wrong because it is bang in the heart of a ski resort that has now become the international benchmark. Val d'Isère, Davos, St Moritz, Cortina, St Anton – each of these world-class resorts has had its turn as the pinnacle of development and facilities; now the baton has passed to Whistler. With two gigantic mountains and some of the fastest lifts in the world, the ski possibilities are awe-inspiring. The only downside to skiing Whistler is that the slopes close relatively early. But with eighty-seven restaurants in town offering everything from Thai to Indian to French to Italian to Mexican to Japanese to Korean, there's no shortage of culinary options. As a resort, Whistler has attained an unusual equilibrium: the choice of ski pistes by day is numerically equivalent to the choice of restaurants by night.

address The Summit Lodge, 4359 Main Street, Whistler, BC Canada, V0N 1B4
t +1 (604) 932 2778 **f** +1 (604) 932 2716 **e** reservations@summitlodge.com
room rates from Cdn $159

hotel dom

The sign says 'Welcome to Saas-Fee – pearl of the Alps'. Even before you have taken in the words, you find yourself facing the largest carpark you have ever seen. Saas-Fee is a car-free village, and this Orwellian giant on the edge of town is their way making quite sure you can't succumb to the temptation to sneak that little Fiat Punto in just quickly to unload your skis. Once you have adjusted to the military scale of the operation, you begin to appreciate that good old Swiss talent for organization. The top floor of the parking station is the arrival floor, where – like a scene from Luc Besson's *Fifth Element* – all cars are guided by 'Swiss Alpine carpark guides' to one of a hundred-odd arrival bays. On every third pillar there's a brightly coloured courtesy phone for you to call your hotel and announce your arrival. Once disgorged of occupants and equipment, your car is taken away by a carpark assistant deep into the labyrinthine megalopolis to be deposited for the duration of your holiday. Judging by the immaculate smoothness of the procedure, the Saas-Fee authorities have been refining it for quite some time. Back at your waiting spot, guides come by with trays of plastic beakers of *Gluhwein* (mountain mulled wine), and before you can say Holy Heidi

Batman, a little electric car bearing the name of your hotel pulls up noiselessly. Skis go on the roof, people and luggage go on the back, and off you go along the picturesque little Hansel and Gretel streets of Saas-Fee. The contrast between chocolate-box Alpine hamlet and Robocop carpark is mind-boggling.

The theme of contrast continues with Hotel Dom. Named after the highest mountain entirely within Switzerland, it also happens to be situated directly opposite the *Dom* – the town church – which, although bang in the middle of this classic Swiss Alpine village, is a modern structure. Hotel Dom, on the outside at least, is another historic building – not a spectacular gem, but a passably handsome turn-of-the-century affair. Inside it's a different story. Instead of timber panelling, etched glass and lace tablecloths there's a piano suspended on the wall by steel cables, a bright yellow fireplace, the odd piece of one-off design furniture, black and white cowhide, and banks of computer screens. And all that's just the lobby. The restaurant has director's chairs in everything from Laura Ashley chintz to zebra-patterned terry towelling; the closet in the corridor is covered in *faux* leopardskin, a bit of old wooden panelling is painted electric blue….

Cowhide and small indoor plants are not out of place in the Alps, but they don't normally appear in this configuration

In the car-free, chocolate-box village of Saas-Fee, everything is old – everything except the town church or *Dom*

Electric blue panelling is one more element of the quirky scheme that expresses Dom's board-riding culture

Compared with the rest of the hotel, the bedrooms are relatively plain and simple – even boarders need a good night's sleep

Drink, dance and shop: the Popcorn Bar is a hangout by day, party venue by night, and also the site of the gear shop

Eccentric and eclectic, Dom is also experimental. These crate chairs are straight from the artist's studio

Hotel Dom's interior is a wild and wildly uncoordinated affair that initially left me grasping for a definition. But then it all became clear: this is a *snowboard* hotel. It's not just the riotous eclecticism or the stylistic irreverence; Hotel Dom's boarder culture is also evident in the laid-back, utterly relaxed attitude – not exactly what you would expect in Switzerland. Nobody seems to be in a hurry, including the staff, so if you are used to perfect Swiss efficiency, be warned – this is probably not the place to be timing the receptionist's check-out rates on the new Tag Heuer Cronograph you picked up tax-free down the road.

The snowboard cult status is completed by the hotel's ultra-hip Popcorn Bar. Most of the town's boarders hang out here at some time during the day and definitely late at night. Not only does it have the obligatory collection of old petrol pumps, Coca Cola signs and other Americana bric-a-brac, it also shares the space with a very happening gear shop. It's a great idea – after a few Coronas that new pair of Oakley goggles suddenly don't seem so expensive after all.

By comparison, the rooms are oddly plain. All have a PlayStation and CD and minidisk player, but their design formula is more recognizably Swiss: white linen eiderdowns, plain pine floors, white bathroom. I guess even the most diehard, rip-all-day, party-all-night boarder (and skier) still wants an uncomplicated room to crash in at night.

And what about the skiing? Like its neighbour, Zermatt, Saas-Fee is a glacier resort. Although not as high or as expansively developed, Saas-Fee offers plenty in terms of very long runs, and because of its altitude – lifts take you to 3,800 metres (12,500 feet) – it's also very snow-safe. But the most remarkable thing about Saas-Fee's mountains is not something you notice until you get higher on the second of the two cable cars. This region, with its successive rows of perfectly shaped triangular peaks, looks more like a Toblerone than anywhere I have ever been.

---

address Hotel Dom, 3906 Saas-Fee, Switzerland

t +41 (27) 957 5101 **f** +41 (27) 957 2300 **e** relax@uniquedom.com

room rates from SFr 79

hotel biner

Sooner or later every skier dreams of Zermatt, the highest skiable place outside the Himalayas. Exactly how high is it? The cable car takes you to the peak of the Kleine Matterhorn, opposite the Matterhorn proper, at a rarefied altitude of 4,000 metres-plus (13,000 feet). To get some perspective on that, consider that Zermatt's summer season skiing terrain offers more pure vertical than the largest, best-known resorts in North America *in winter*. In June, July and August, skiable terrain on the Zermatt glacier starts above 4,000 metres and ends just above 2,000 metres (6,500 feet) – that's a vertical of 2 km or some 7,000 feet. Aspen's biggest vertical in the winter is just under 6,000 feet. In the winter you can add another kilometre to Zermatt's skiable vertical. It also has the diversity and variety typical of European linked resorts. There are different mountains to explore, and given enough time, you can ski into parts of Italy that would take a full day to reach by car. No wonder this picturesque Swiss town attracts skiers from all over the world.

Zermatt has also long had the advantage of being a car-free town. Anyone arriving by car has to leave it in Täsch and then proceed either by train or by taxi. These days, however, there are so many electric cars in Zermatt that even

if the town is car-free, it certainly isn't traffic-free. What's more, this is not really the tiny Swiss *Dorf* that the tourism services would have you believe. True, Zermatt has plenty of charm, and the ambience is unmistakably Alpine-Swiss, but a tiny town it is not.

By the turn of the twentieth century Zermatt was already a major destination for summer Alpinists, as it still is. The town's famous guardian, the Matterhorn, made it a magnet for mountain tourists long before skiing's mass-popularity. Given such history, Zermatt naturally has its share of grand old hotels. As with most places in Switzerland, if you are prepared to pay enough money, you will find a very good place to stay. But interesting accommodation without breaking the bank is another story. Usually, as the number of stars drop, so do the facilities, the quality and the personality. Not so with Hotel Biner. Located a stone's-throw from the railway station, Biner is the new face of Zermatt tourism: young, groovy, and not so enamoured with tradition as to be held back by it. From the outside it doesn't look so different from most buildings in Zermatt: slanted roof, small windows, a bit of timber, four or five storeys high – charming, but nothing new.

In contrast to most of Biner's interiors, the restaurant is a reassuringly familiar space of old timber and small windows

Car-free Zermatt is a popular destination for serious Alpinists. The surrounding peaks are some of the highest in Europe

Flouting convention, the lobby is furnished with an ensemble of hanging hammocks

Hotel Biner houses a spa complex that includes a sauna, a pool, a steam room and, of course, a jacuzzi

Some guestrooms are like loft spaces in the snow. Better yet, the view is of the Matterhorn

The indoor underground pool is big enough to swim laps – not normally a feature of an affordable three-star hotel

Inside, from the moment you enter, it's clear there is a modern mentality at work. Jürg Biner took over the hotel when his parents retired and immediately started to put his stamp on the place. On the top floor, the rooms are blond lofts – large, light spaces with a bath in the middle and a postcard view of the Matterhorn. At this point, there are just a handful of these lofts, but the plans are for more on other floors in the near future. Not that the other rooms could be called old-fashioned: white walls, modern art and pine furniture define a scheme that repeats in the raised dining room and the hanging lobby, an area set aside for a collection of unusual sitting hammocks – a particular hit with anyone under fourteen. Adults are also well catered to with a splendid spa complex that includes a substantial swimming pool, a hot tub section, a large glass-sided sauna and a very funky nightclub-style steamroom.

Even the ski and boot room is equipped in a fashion normally reserved to five-star establishments. The ski room, as one would expect, leads directly outside, thus no clunking around the lobby in ski boots, and the boot room features a state-of-the-art drying and deodorizing machine. Not at Biner will your ski boots smell like a slab of soft French cheese.

But aside from the streamlined design and luxury facilities, Biner also has that chalet ambience so important to a ski vacation. The place is casual but efficient, and all the guests seem to be in terrific form: happy and smiling, perhaps because Hotel Biner is such a good find. Or maybe it's because they have taken part in the Luttman-Johnson race, the world's most spectacular pub crawl. Zermatt may be the only ski resort in the world that has an entire guidebook dedicated to its mountain restaurants (there are over thirty of them). Every January competitors ski from one to the next 'clocking up forkage and slurpage', as they say. The winner is determined by a bizarrely complex formula, though nobody takes much notice as this is one race in which the Olympic creed – 'taking part is what counts' – really applies.

---

address Hotel Biner, Ch-3920 Zermatt, Switzerland

t +41 (27) 966 5666 **f** +41 (27) 966 5667 **e** info@hotel-biner-zermatt.ch

room rates from SFr 75

HIP™
HOTELS

First published in paperback in the United States of America in 2002 by Thames & Hudson Inc., 500 Fifth Avenue, New York, New York 10110

thamesandhudsonusa.com

Library of Congress Catalog Card Number 2002100550
ISBN 0-500-28375-3

Printed and bound in Singapore by CS Graphics

Acknowledgments
Photography by Herbert Ypma, with the exception of The Brand, Riders Palace and Le St Joseph, supplied courtesy of the hotels.

Designed by Maggi Smith

In memory of my father, who put me on a pair of skis when I was still young enough to think it was normal.